How To
SCORE
GOALS

How To SCORE GOALS

MALCOLM MACDONALD

with Martin Samuel

Photography by
Bed Radford

Graphics by
Paul Buckle

The Kingswood Press

Published 1985 by
The Kingswood Press
Kingswood, Tadworth, Surrey
(an imprint of William Heinemann Ltd)

Typeset by Alacrity Phototypesetters,
Banwell Castle, Weston-super-Mare
Printed and bound in Great Britain by
William Clowes Ltd, Beccles and London

0 434 98064 1

Contents

1 · Are you a Goalscorer?

I suppose the obvious response to that question is: "Well, what **is** a goalscorer?"

I spent the best part of a career mulling that over, and to some extent it still puzzles me. I think the simplest answer would be to say he's the hero or the villain.

Goalscorers are the extremists of football. In the eyes of their team-mates, their manager, their coach, the crowd and the Press, they do one of two things: they score or they miss.

If they score they get the congratulatory slaps on the back, the applause, the headlines and the warm grins in the changing-room afterwards. But if they miss, they receive the groans, the moans and the criticism in the papers.

As I said: hero or villain. If you're not in one of those categories after every match, then you're not a goalscorer. You might be a forward, or an attacking midfield player, but you're *not* the man with the responsibility for scoring most of your team's goals.

The most important thing about being a goalscorer is appreciating that you have to be the villain some of the time. Because to score,

you must miss — no-one is going to bury every opportunity that comes his way.

To take this argument to its ultimate conclusion: when you miss an open goal, do you have the confidence to dismiss it and not allow it to affect your game? Can you keep going until finally a chance goes in?

The media talk of "dry spells", when no matter what you do, you cannot score a goal. Every goalscorer has them and it is vital that he retains his self-belief and is on hand to miss again and again until the spell is broken. The secret is to tell yourself: "Whatever else may happen, I am *going* to score a goal."

To do this you have to be greedy, and invariably you'll be criticised by team-mates. You have to ignore easy passing opportunities to take the riskier option of shooting.

My first season for Newcastle was 1971-72 and in the opening game at Crystal Palace I had a nightmare. In the second match,

The photographs on these pages, and the next two, feature David Speedie, the young Chelsea and Scotland striker. He has had a dramatic rise to prominence, after starting his career with Darlington in the Fourth Division ... and I think the photographs go some way towards explaining why.

They illustrate a number of the attributes and qualities I look for in a goalscorer.

On this page, for example, Speedie shows his willingness to go flat-out for every ball in the box ...to try and get in a header or shot even though the odds are heavily stacked against him succeeding.

against Tottenham, things began to get better — the Newcastle lads were playing in a way that suited me — but I still didn't score. In my third outing, against Liverpool, I got a hat-trick.

I continued to strike at regular intervals until, two months later, my forward partner John Tudor approached me after training one day and said: "You are the most selfish so and so I have ever seen on a football field!"

"I know, John," I replied!

He probably meant that as an insult — I have never been sure — but I always regarded it as a compliment.

My theory was this: if I had the ball at my feet and could see a midfield player in a better scoring position, I was nonetheless better off shooting than knocking the ball to him. I felt that I was more liable to score from a difficult position, than a midfielder was when presented with an easy chance. Many players are "shot-shy" and will only have a pop when they are certain the ball will go in.

The man who taught me to be, "a greedy so

3

and so" was Harry Haslam at Luton.

Harry told me: "Go and practice scoring goals" — and took me to an empty room above the club sports shop. It was a long room, about six yards wide, with a stairwell in the middle and two blank walls at each end.

"Here," he said, and gave me a "Johnny Giles" ball. It was a light, plastic ball, with black dots and the names of various English and Scottish League teams in the white spaces.

The ball was ridiculously bouncy and would fly at all angles — but never the true one — making it very hard to control.

I used to strike the ball against one end of the room and, as it rebounded off, get it, turn and shoot. Harry taught me that, as a goal-scorer, this should be uppermost in my mind: *get it, turn and shoot.*

I practiced for hours; not until I had worked up a sweat but until my ears were ringing with the sound of that ball slamming against the clubhouse wall!

But Harry's words remained evermore in my mind. When you get the ball at your feet, with your back to goal, go on the half-turn and whip a shot in. I can honestly say that I would never have got half my goals had it not been for advice like that.

I would turn and shoot and the centre-halves would block it; I would turn and shoot and the ball would hit the corner-flag; I would turn and shoot and the ball would settle comfortably in row Z of the stand. Every time this happened my team-mates would yell: "For God's sake, Mal, play it simple, lay it off!"

But when the ball hit the net they were the first to say: "What a great goal!"

Once again, you're the hero or the villain. Unless you're prepared to take a lot of "stick" — mentally and physically — you won't be a goalscorer.

Not that goalscoring is simply a case of walking out on to a football field with a pig-

These photographs, of Speedie in action against Arsenal, prompt the thought that the Gunners' defenders must have been delighted to hear the final whistle!

Speedie is the type of striker who tends to wear down opponents, both physically and mentally.

Left, Arsenal's Brian Talbot (now Watford) is on the receiving end of the sort of determined challenge for which he himself is renowned. Right, Speedie, cool-headed, alert and ready to pounce on the ball like a lithe cat, portrays the classic goal-scorer's pose in the hurly-burly of the six-yard box.

5

Being a goalscorer can be a demoralising experience. He will make numerous runs into scoring positions, without ever getting the ball, and generally, he is going to miss considerably more chances than he converts.

That's why nothing can compare with the feeling you get when the ball does go in the net.

The expression on Speedie's face in this photograph says it all!

headed attitude — you've got to be able to play.

You don't have to be Michel Platini — in fact, many of the world's greatest strikers were generally indifferent footballers, technically — but you do need a requisite number of skills to be capable at your job.

You have to be able to control a ball, to head it and to shoot with a reasonable degree of accuracy.

More specialist skills include the ability to anticipate a scoring chance, to lose your marker in order to get a shot in, to position yourself in accordance with the state of general play and to utilise your strengths as a means of hiding your weaknesses.

Finally, you need to have the correct

attitude, to yourself, your team-mates and your opponents.

I will deal with all of these in greater detail later in the book, but if I give a brief outline, you should be able to answer that all-important question: Am I a goalscorer?

To take the more general skills first ...

Control

Your control has to be good in order to retain possession. It is no use team-mates feeding a striker who loses the ball to his marker every time.

Admittedly, the centre-forward is the only man on the field "licensed" to lose possession — but only by having a shot saved, or go wide.

Once the ball is in your control you have three options: (i) turn and run at the centre-half (ii) turn and shoot (iii) lay the ball off and run to find a new angle for the return pass.

Heading

A common misconception is that height determines your heading ability.

What rubbish! You may be small, but if you're quick you can move across your marker and get in a header unchallenged. Obviously, a striker who is 5 ft. 6 in. will have to work harder at this aspect of his game than someone who is 6 ft., but success can be achieved.

The best example of the benefits of hard work is Kevin Keegan. Kevin is 5 ft. 8 in., but scored a remarkable amount of goals with his head, simply because he attained great power, so that when he did get there, he made it count.

He also made himself quick, and got his positioning right. Thus, although he might not outjump his marker, he would get to the cross first.

Shooting

The most important aspect of shooting is accuracy. You don't need a Bobby Charlton-type blaster to score. In fact, one of the scruffiest kickers of the ball I have ever seen was West Germany's Gerd Muller. Gordon Davies, the Welsh International striker who was with me at Fulham, is also a poor kicker of the ball, but, like Muller, he is accurate, and that's all-important.

Contrary to popular belief, few goalscorers "pick their spot", as the commentators say. That's nonsense — often your "spot" is picked for you by the position of the goal-keeper or the defence.

Often it is as vague as shooting to one half of the goal, or to the right or left of the keeper. Sometimes you just see the white posts and let fly!

If a shot is well-placed, it doesn't need to burst the net, so always aim for accuracy more than power. Once you have achieved the first, the second is likely to follow.

You need to be generally competent at all these skills. They will no doubt improve with practice, but if you find that after two years your control is still not all it should be, don't worry. There are plenty of ways to beat a defence.

Now we come to the more specific goal-scoring requirements. The requirements needed to burst through a defence, into a position to receive a ball that will best suit your talents.

Losing Your Marker

This, of course, is the first step needed to score regularly and the most important thing is to constantly test the man put on the field to stop you.

"Drag" your marker into a false position to see if he'll follow you. If he doesn't, great — you are unmarked!

Always remember that the only person who is aware of your next move is *you*. Never let the defender settle. Keep checking, keep dummying and if you still can't get away, use the old Jimmy Greaves ploy.

Jimmy would just stand on the edge of the area. Defenders hate that, because they know something is coming but they're unsure what. Then Jimmy would dart, and often as not the ball would come for him to put it away.

Look at any photographs or films of Jimmy's goals. Half the time a perplexed defender can be seen in the background, with an expression on his face that says: "Now, how did he do that? I had him here a moment ago."

Obviously, a forward's thinking changes once inside the penalty area. There, you *never* stand still, because once you are motionless you offer as good a defensive body as an attacking body.

Once again, there are different ways to create your space and I will explain these in detail later.

Positioning

The way in which you lose your marker is frequently dictated by the pattern of play adopted by your team, and it is very important for a goalscorer to know how to work in various formations.

9

4-4-2, 4-3-3 and 4-2-4 require different strategies from the goalscorer and it is vital that you create an understanding with your forward partner or partners.

Usually the relationship between two strikers is very similar to that between a comedy double act. The goalscorer is the comic, his partner the feed, and you have to know how to get the best out of your feed.

Anticipation

To strip a goalscorer's instinct down to its most basic level would be to say that it is simply "gambling."

You gamble that the ball will arrive at a certain position on the field and, if it doesn't, you have to shrug your shoulders and wait for the next opportunity.

You gamble on rebounds, on the ball bouncing out of a goalkeeper's hands, on a team-mate's shot going off target so that you can nip in near a post to prod it home, on a defender failing to clear. Indeed, you gamble on *anything* so long as you think it will give you a goal.

Allan Clarke once said that there is no such thing as a "lucky" goal, and I agree. If a pass takes four rebounds and finally reaches you a yard out at the far post for the easiest tap-in of your life, it is just as valuable as a 25-yard volley.

My belief always was: "Well, if I hadn't been there it wouldn't have been a goal. And I certainly wasn't there due to luck!"

I played in an FA Cup semi-final for Arsenal against Orient at Stamford Bridge in 1978. We won 3-0 and I got two of the goals, through deflections off defenders.

The first shot was going wide of the far post when it struck a full-back, thus wrong-footing the keeper, and crept in. The second was a carbon copy, except the defender slid in to put it over his own line.

After the match, Brian Moore, the commentator for London Weekend Television, said I had no right to claim those goals. But I have always maintained that had I not shot at goal the ball would never have gone in. Anyway, my name is in the record books for all to see!

Similarly, playing for Arsenal against West Bromwich Albion, I needed one goal for my hat-trick.

The ball was played through the inside-right channel, and I was challenged by the West Brom defender Derek Statham, who got to the ball first and was about to make a clearance. But I kicked the back of his foot just as his boot was about to make contact — and this propelled the ball at great speed into the top corner!

I immediately claimed a hat-trick.

The point is, you've got to try and score any way you can. On this occasion, the referee was satisfied that the goal was legitimate.

In this situation, don't forget to hold up your arm to let everyone know it was *your* goal.

Anticipation, the goalscorer's "radar" — call it what you will — is perhaps the hardest part of a striker's make-up to master.

It needs constant work, studying your team-mates and your opponents, because only by knowing them will you have any idea where the ball will eventually turn up.

Playing To Strengths/Attitude

Even the greatest of players has weaknesses, and it is important for you to analyse your own.

If you are tall and good in the air, it is pointless your team-mates playing balls behind the defence in the hope of you running onto them. To go to the other extreme, if you are small and quick, it is a waste of time your midfielders playing high balls which force you into a battle in the air with a centre-half twice your size.

Not all strengths and weaknesses are as clear-cut as this, but you will greatly benefit from analysing yourself and then telling the players around you of your needs.

Too many midfielders try to play in inches, squeezing balls through tiny gaps. I always told colleagues: "Play in yards. I don't mind doing the extra running as long as it will enable me to create space."

In this respect, the best man I ever played with was Newcastle's Terry Hibbitt. When it came to creating chances for his strikers, Terry's criteria were: 1. the ball must beat the defender 2. it must not be too close to the goalkeeper.

Often his passes were so perfect that they would elude my marker *and* tempt the goalkeeper out of position, under the impression that he could get to the ball first. He rarely did, and I usually collected a goal. Terry and I worked this move hundreds of times.

But you have to tell your team-mates what to do ...

For example, one important aspect of passing — particularly as far as a striker is concerned — is that you receive a ball on the same foot with which it has been delivered to you, i.e. right foot to right foot; left foot to left foot. It's difficult to explain, but basically it automatically puts the striker's body in between the ball and his marker, and thus helps him retain possession.

A goalscorer has to make demands on the

manager, the coach, his fellow players, but most of all, on himself.

You must demand a hat-trick in every game, and if you score two, you must be disappointed, but resolve to get three in the next match.

You must say: "To hell with everything else, I am here to score goals, and that is all I want to do!"

I once sat and counted how many times in a match the average goalscorer touches the ball. It was frightening. If you get six different touches, with the slightest possibility of a crack at goal, you have done well. Therefore, I set myself a target: for every six touches, I must score one goal.

If I was given the ball at my feet, ten yards outside the area, with my back to the goal and a centre-half breathing down my neck, that was a scoring chance. If all went well, I could turn him and get a shot in.

You must condemn yourself to a life spent studying opponents and team-mates, doing extra training when everyone else has long gone and having a job that you can never get out of your mind.

Those are the personal demands. Now we come to your team-mates.

Naturally, we return to the old battle of strengths versus weaknesses. Many mid-fielders will play the ball *they* want to play — not the one you want to receive. Many will merely "lend" balls, playing them in such a way that you have no option but to return the pass. That way they govern possession.

In the end, I told my colleagues that when they looked up, I would start my run and, having done that, I *must* get the ball.

This might seem an arrogant attitude, but it is the only one if you want to keep scoring.

In the same way, you have to regard the six yard box as *your* patch.

Often, midfielders or defenders will make a run into the area, then stand still if the ball hasn't arrived, in the hope that it soon will.

Anyone who is motionless in the box is "dead meat," so tell them to get the hell out! Otherwise, they will clutter the area and stop the man who is paid to score goals from doing his job.

They won't welcome you intruding on *their* patch, so tell them to pay the same respect to yours.

The greatest goalscorers — men like Jimmy Greaves, Gerd Muller, Ian Rush — tend to operate as totally separate entities from their teams.

They don't get involved in the build-ups, they don't help out in defence, they stand completely outside the pattern of play, until the ball reaches the penalty area. *Then* they come alive. You have to be in the right place at the right time to score goals — and that is a full-time job.

What made me want to do it? It all started at Luton.

It was my first season with Luton 1969-70 — they had signed me from Fulham for £18,000 — and the following day we were set to play our opening game of the season, at home to Barrow.

Manager Alec Stock walked into our dressing-room and told us: "Gentlemen, we are going to win promotion to Division Two, and I'll tell you how we're going to do it."

He then proceeded to spell out how many points were needed and therefore how many games had to be won, and the maximum number we could lose.

To get that number of points we needed a certain number of goals and, one by one, Alec went through the team, informing each individual just how many were expected to come from him.

Finally, he came to my forward partners. From Graham French he required 12, and from Lawrie Sheffield 18. I was left till last.

I had only recently been converted to centre-forward, after spending most of my career at full-back. I saw my target as about 15.

"And from you, young man," Alec said, looking me up and down, "I want 30 goals!"

I almost fell through my seat! I couldn't believe it! Thirty goals was double my expectations, and I thought the task impossible. But Alec simply turned his back — the matter was closed.

With this load hanging over my head, I stepped out to play Barrow. When I returned after 90 minutes we had won 3-0, but I had not knocked a single goal from my target.

I had rarely felt so dejected. That total was a matter of personal pride, and I had failed my first test.

Suffice to say, Luton got their promotion, and I missed my target. By one!

The team's achievement meant little to me. I even went to Alec Stock and apologised. "Well show me you can do it next year, young man,' was his reply. (I did — I got 31!)

But even though Alec ruined what should have been a highpoint in my career, I have never stopped thanking him for doing so.

Harry Haslam taught me the virtues of "get it, turn and shoot", but Alec made me realise that goalscoring was my life. He wanted nothing else from me but goals — and how I got them did not matter.

Before that I had been a *player*. Alec made me a *goalscorer*.

Now, I hope to do the same for you ...

2 · Control

This chapter could just as easily be titled "Get it, turn and shoot" because, for a goal-scorer, controlling the ball should only form the means to an end of having a pop at the target.

Whether by running at the defence and goalkeeper or by letting fly from some 25 yards, a goal attempt should always be looked upon as your No. 1 aim.

Unfortunately it has become increasingly rare in today's game, for two simple reasons:
1. The negative attitude of many coaches, who tell centre-forwards "to play the way they are facing". In other words, when receiving the ball with your back to goal, they expect you return it to your midfielders.
2. The unavoidable fact that you're going to get kicked up in the air 50 per cent of the time!

Centre-halves are quite happy for you to adopt the coach's methods, because those methods pose no threat. The ball goes out of the danger zone and the centre half has time to re-position for the second through-ball. There is little chance of him being caught for pace.

But the one thing they cannot stand is a man who will turn and run at them, or turn

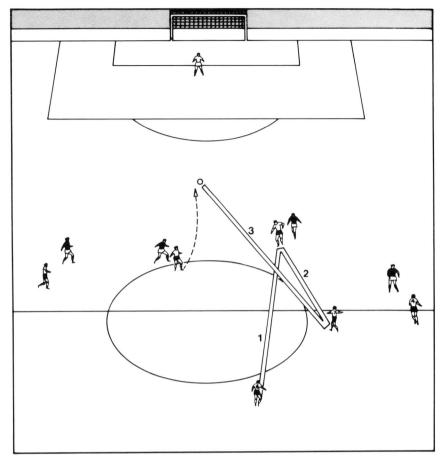

and fire a shot. Once they realise your intention they will clout you as soon as the ball reaches your feet. My obsession with turning my marker probably accounts for my early retirement, at the age of 29. If I had been happy to take the "easy" option, I would possibly have lasted into my 30s — but I wouldn't have scored half as many goals!

My style and beliefs never failed to provoke a do-or-die attitude from my opponent. But I, too, would throw all caution to the wind.

Occasionally, I would spend days on a treatment table after a particularly bad pasting. I certainly counted the cost in terms of bruises and aching legs on a Saturday

This illustration will please the numerous coaches who insist that strikers should "play the way they are facing."

I am not necessarily against that – sometimes it's the best way – but I think there has been too much emphasis on the point, causing a lot of front men to become too predictable.

I prefer to adopt a more positive attitude – in this situation, I would be more inclined to encourage a striker to turn with the ball and go for goal, rather than lay it off. As I kept doing as a player!

17

night. But, to me, all this was justified by my goal tally.

If your hunger for goals isn't that great or you don't have enough confidence to turn a defender or you don't like getting kicked, then forget any ideas of being the next Jimmy Greaves.

You will have to go against the advice of your coach and your team-mates, and be selfish. You will have to practice, practice, practice and some days take a right beating for little or nothing. But if all you want is your name on a scoresheet, then "get it, turn and shoot" is the best advice you'll ever have.

Strangely few coaches seem to realise that the man best positioned to turn and run at a defence is the centre-forward, because once you have eluded your marker, you often have a clear 20-yard sprint at goal.

Nowadays, most of the attacking runs are made from midfield. Ludicrous! Those operating behind the forward line often have three or four defenders still to beat.

Of course, attacking runs by midfield players are necessary, but not as the main point of attack.

So never fail to chance a turn. Remember, the goalscorer is the only man in the team licensed to lose possession; and, if you are scoring regularly, the negative arguments of coaches are proved wrong.

The first step is to demand the "right" ball from your midfielders. Everything must be played in at pace, because a ball hit gently, or one that bobbles along the ground, will put you in hospital!

Having made that clear you can then consider your options when the ball is on its way.

Obviously, there are times when you have to lay it off, then turn and run for goal in the hope of receiving a return pass. But your primary objective should be to turn and run at the defence, or shoot!

There are many variations when attempting to round your marker, all of which will be dealt with later in the chapter, but here are a few simple guidelines.

The way in which you turn — inside him or outside him — should be dictated by the position of the defender.

You must have a solid standing foot nearest the centre-half, and the other in a position to spring around him to finish in the direction your shot will be aimed.

Balance is an important part of this manoeuvre, and I found the best way to achieve it was to lean into the centre-half. That way, you unbalance him by making him the pivot for your own movements.

In most instances, the centre-forward, just before he receives the ball, should be on the point of a half-turn, thus collecting the ball side-on.

Centre-halves are normally big men, so a striker should crouch as low as possible. By achieving a low centre of gravity, you make it difficult for an opponent to knock you over.

But, although your control should be as complete as possible, never forget that it is only the first step on the way to an altogether more important aim — scoring.

These are, of course, merely the general rules, and I will now move on to more specific means of control.

Every move discussed here must be worked at constantly.

By demanding the most from oneself on the training field, an average footballer can be made better, and the good can become great.

But first things first. There are two basic forms of semi-static control . . .

The Inside Turn

Having first leaned against the centre-half, your next aim is to control the ball, moving it a yard away from your body.

The ball should never "sit" at the bottom of an imaginary line down from your chin where the centre-half can nip around you and get at it to make his clearance. By controlling three feet from your body, keeping your body directly between the defender and the ball, you (a) take the ball out of his reach, (b) take it wide enough to get a shot in or peel off with the ball in your possession.

By keeping the ball from the greedy grasp of your opponent, he has no alternative but to step off you, putting himself at your mercy, or commit a blatant foul, putting himself at the mercy of the referee.

Now we move to where the ball is arriving and you have shaped to control it a yard away from you.

You gain momentum to receive the ball by pushing off the centre-half, thus rendering him even more vulnerable.

As the ball arrives, turn around the centre-

half, and use your standing foot to come across and block off his tackle. He is now powerless to stop you. To get a tackle in, he cannot help but commit a foul and, if he doesn't do that, you will be in a position to strike the ball or run with it.

But the main thing is to be shaped and positioned before the ball arrives. Obviously, it is foolish to attempt this manoeuvre with the wrong through-pass, because you'll end up on your backside with the ball 60 yards up the field!

Apart from the fact that I am demonstrating the inside turn, what else have you noticed about the photo-sequence on these pages?

The answer is that the ball is on my favourite left foot – and I'm doing what always came naturally to me. Remember: "GET IT, TURN, SHOOT!"

The Outside Turn

The alternative to going goalside (the inside turn) is simply going non-goalside, the long way round, in order to widen the angle.

You can kid that you are going to turn inside, by going through the relevant shaping motions but, at the last moment, change the angle of the foot receiving the ball and use the centre-half as a springboard to push off and go in the opposite direction.

The centre-half will already be moving to one side (in this case the wrong one!) and will be further thrown off-balance by your movements and body contact.

Your spin should look very much like that of a diver, going backwards off the board with a half turn.

If you have chosen to run at goal, your next movement should be to push the ball on with your standing foot, continuing the run and

then making your "controlling" foot the foot of acceleration.

These are the most simple forms of controlling a ball, but even greater success can be achieved by utilising the hundreds of variations. Some are simple, others not so ...

Until now, we have always presumed that the centre-half is in close attention, standing directly behind you. (See diagram on page 27)

But this is not always the case. Sometimes, the defender will stand slightly off — although still goalside — and this is something you can use to great advantage.

For example, if the ball is hit to you diagonally from a wide position and you move towards it, you will have enough space to begin the turn just before the ball arrives. Catch it on the instep of your inner foot and turn to face the centre-half with the ball in full control. Nothing scares an opponent more! The momentum of your spin means

that it is unthinkable for him to commit himself, and you are now perfectly positioned for a run at goal with only the centre-half to beat. This is the ideal form of control for a ball arriving diagonally from a wide position as, after the turn, the ball should lie at your inner foot, ready to be cut inside the defender.

Like most forms of control, this movement can be reversed. The ball from the centre of the field, moving outside, can be controlled and spun with the outer foot, ready to be taken wide of the centre-half.

The top pros have some brilliant variations to these moves. Trevor Francis, for example, is always worth watching in this respect.

These movements have so far been made when receiving the so-called "perfect ball" — the one that comes at just the right height and pace for your form of control.

But there are occasions when the centre-

Taking a ball hit diagonally from a wide position (in this case from the left of the photo). It's me versus Les Strong, the former Fulham defender. As you can see, I am making it extremely difficult for Les to get to the ball, through the position of my arms and body. I am looking to create a yard of space, and then cut the ball inside him with my inner foot.

25

A great example of holding off a defender, by Mike Fillery of Queens Park Rangers in a match against Tottenham. Apart from using the arms to block the defender's path to the ball, Fillery can also "feel" where he is and which way he is moving.

forward is caught slightly out of position, or in two minds.

For instance, he has pushed off the defender to receive the ball, only to find that he could easily reach the ball.

When that happens, the striker has no alternative but to control the ball with his trailing leg, and bring the receiving foot back into the body so that the angle of the ball is changed and controlled into the standing foot. Now you are in a position to move off and attack the centre-half.

Your opponent has three options. He can move forward, allowing you to turn in the opposite direction and round him. He can stand still and wait for you — a hideous mistake as your momentum should be easily

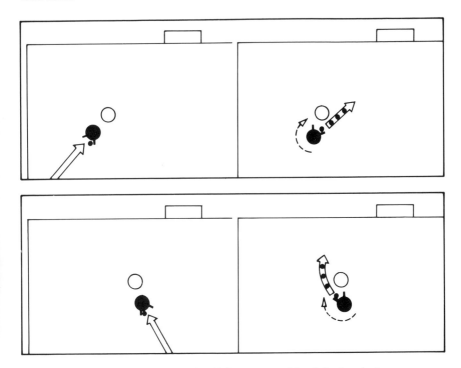

Here are two of the numerous ways in which you can punish a defender who has given you too much space. (A) an ideal method of turning with a ball played to you diagonally from a wide position. (B) Turning with a ball hit to you in a wide position from the centre of the field.

An extraordinary Trevor Francis variation on (A). The difference is that the ball is coming to him from a different position, and his turn is considerably greater. He's got it off to such a fine art that he makes it almost impossible to counter. He takes the ball on the inside of his "inner" foot, and shapes to take it on the outside of the defender. But he switches the ball to the outside of his other foot and, swivelling around, beats the defender on the inside.

27

enough to go past him. Or he can back peddle — another mistake, as you are gathering speed all the time and, if he dithers too long without commiting himself, he will eventually run out of pitch.

If you have any doubts at all about gaining control and possession, then as a rule of thumb, always move towards the ball; never be caught waiting for it. Get to it before there is a chance of interception.

Often you will be expected to move on to a through-ball at speed, and it is vital that you are capable of controlling a ball on the run — because if a midfielder's pass splits the opposing defence, he won't be particularly happy if you dribble it into touch or let it through your legs.

The most important thing is to control in your stride, anticipating the ball and adjusting your prior steps accordingly.

Your first priority is to "kill" the pass. Overweight your control and the ball will

rebound strongly from your foot, under-
weight it and the ball will pass beneath your
feet. You should already be judging the pace
of the pass so that, when it arrives, you will be
able to deal with the ball.

Secondly you must judge the angle in
which you want to run, once the ball is at
your feet. Remember how hard it is to change
direction at speeds of 10-15 m.p.h. Cars and
motorbikes have wheels, you have only 12
studs, and falling flat on your face with the
goal begging is an extremely embarrassing
experience.

So far I have presumed that you are faced
with a clear dash at goal, but it is likely a
defender will be approaching and shaping to
tackle.

In these cases it is best to knock the ball
past him and control beyond. At all other
times, control should be achieved in your
second stride.

Nearer the goal, your priority has to be to

*What to do when you
have to really stretch
behind to bring a pass
under control.*

control and shoot in two, quick motions. The inside turn and outside turn and their subtle variations are purely for use 30-40 yards outside your opponents' goal. Once approaching, or inside, the penalty area, you will rarely have time for such complicated procedures.

Awareness counts for everything. Sum up the position of the defence quickly and get in a shot hoping the goalkeeper is caught out of position.

When given a diagonal pass, an alternative to a first-time shot is to take weight off the pace of the ball, but still allow it to move on its original line. The shot is thus made with the controlling foot. Again, it is vital to perfect the control and shot into one fluent movement.

If you can imagine the penalty area as a clock-face, with the goalkeeper representing the hour, and the centre of the "D" the half hour, you will find that by studying all the matches you either watch or play in that the vast majority of goals are scored from an angle either between 20 and 10 to the hour or ten and twenty past the hour. Rarely are goals scored from around the half hour, and even more seldom the angles near the dead-ball line. So work to gain your shooting position in the more favourable angles whenever possible.

The best practice when attempting to perfect the angle of shot is to have a training partner roll a ball at you from every conceivable direction and you striking it from different positions — ie inside left and right, outside left and right and centre-forward. That way, you will be well aware of your capabilities, from all angles.

A further tactic when controlling in and around the box, is to drop your backside onto the centre-half's thigh and virtually "sit" on him.

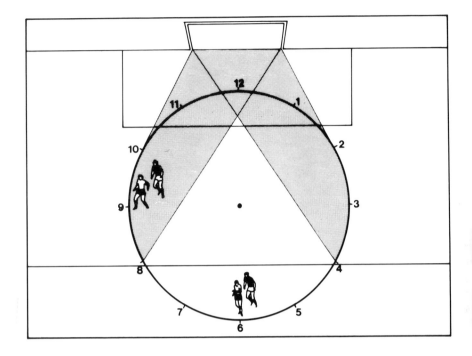

I have already extolled the virtues of the "goalscorer' crouch", and this trick is simply its most logical extension.

By dropping your backside onto his thigh, you render your marker completely motionless. He finds it impossible to move and, if he wants to, will literally shove you off and risk conceding a free-kick or even a penalty!

I have noticed that both commentators and referees rarely interpret this tactic in the way that I do. I believe it to be a foul by the forward, but quite often it is the defender who is penalised — particularly if he backs away and sends the striker sprawling.

An added bonus is that his leg works perfectly as your springboard, giving you a solid pivot base. With practice it even becomes easy to shoot from a sitting or crouching position, particularly when turning on goal.

Look at this "clock" ... and, in particular, the shaded areas. It's in these that most goals are scored.

31

I am virtually sitting on Les Strong's thigh ... and, as the photograph indicates, I am the one who is liable to produce the most telling initial sprint for the ball.

Once you have mastered control with the feet, you can move on to other parts of the body — most importantly, the thigh and chest.

"Killing" the ball with the thigh (top left) and the chest. In both cases, note the manner in which the striker is shielding the ball from the defender.

Thigh control, though easy to explain, is difficult to utilise correctly.

The ball must be killed on impact with a good, solid cushion, and then with the foot, pushed away from the centre-half into space.

Controlling the ball with your chest necessitates a square back and slightly outstretched forward arms, creating a little "hole" for the ball to drop into.

Shield it between your shoulders and your chin, in such a "protective" way so as to prevent the centre half getting a good view of the ball, and nipping in to clear it.

Make sure it drops from chest to feet, giving you the time to act as you please. As it falls off your chest you can use feet control to spin off the centre-half, if he is standing back and move away with the ball in your possession.

If he is tight, it could even be worth shielding the ball, pressing your weight against him and swinging around him at the moment of control.

The only time the ball should be allowed to pop up off the chest is if you're attempting to get a volley in. In this case always tee the ball up to the left or right of the defender — so he is too far away to intercept — and judge at which height you want to strike the ball. The possibilities are endless — anything from a low volley on the turn to an overhead bicycle kick.

Almost all forms of control mentioned so far have been of the type often seen at grounds around the country — or at least they used to be!

The opening photo of this sequence (page 34) shows me preparing to take a ball on the chest. But then, Les Strong makes physical contact, letting me know exactly where he is. More importantly, he has let me know that he is close enough for me to both control the ball and turn him in the same movement.

It's surprising how many defenders make the mistake of actually touching the men they are marking in these situations.

I remember I noticed this with some of Fulham's defenders when I became manager of the club. "You're making it easier for opposing forwards," I told them. "You've got to keep them guessing."

Magic from Keegan.

Some of my contemporaries adopted more unorthodox methods of beating a defence. Here are some examples ...

RODNEY MARSH, of Fulham, Queens Park Rangers, Manchester City and England would kid a centre-half that he was about to lay the ball back, then strike it with the outside of his foot to spin it 270 degrees. He would then turn the remaining 90, and fire a shot on meeting the ball behind his marker's back!

KEVIN KEEGAN of Scunthorpe, Liverpool, SV Hamburg, Southampton, Newcastle and England would dummy to control a ball, but let it run so that he could flick the ball behind his standing leg.

FRANCIS LEE, of Manchester City, Derby County and England, performed a trick that I have never seen repeated.

Franny was a little, barrel-chested man, but one of the cheekiest strikers I have ever seen. On one occasion the ball was played through to him at chest height and Franny jerked his head back and his chest up, knocking the ball over the centre-half's head. He then ran round his opponent and fired sharply into the net.

When discussing these sort of tricks, I am instantly reminded of a match for Arsenal against Ipswich, George Armstrong crossed from a wing and I began to move towards the ball.

The centre-half followed me and, at the last minute, I opened my legs and let the ball through. David Price was following up and he scored easily.

The golden lesson to be learnt from these — and all other — forms of control is: be aware of your opponent.

Unless you are in actual physical contact with him and can sense his direction of movement or intentions, make sure you know his position and distance from you.

Otherwise he can nip in first and make you feel a fool.

Don't be satisfied with merely competent control — that will get you nowhere if you keep turning into trouble.

One further tip with regards to practice: never practice with good passes and through-balls, always with awkward or hard ones.

Have them knocked with curl, spin and bouncing at unusual heights to make you stretch. Because once you have mastered controlling bad balls, controlling good ones becomes easy.

3 · Shooting

Having learned to control the ball, the next step is to master effective methods of shooting.

It is important to list what you are setting out to achieve, because this is frequently the downfall of prototype goalscorers — and even some at League level.

Too many feel that a shot needs to be so powerful it will burst the net to have a chance of counting. Therefore, as they make contact with the ball, their head goes up and the shot balloons over the bar, or the mis-contact of the boot on the ball causes the shot to go wide.

Left, the WRONG way to shoot. Look how sloppy I appear. I am not looking at the ball, am leaning back and the end-product is a shot which is almost certainly going to lack power and will certainly go too high. This page, the RIGHT way. Eyes fixed firmly on the ball, the body over it – the whole technique is much more compact and streamlined isn't it?

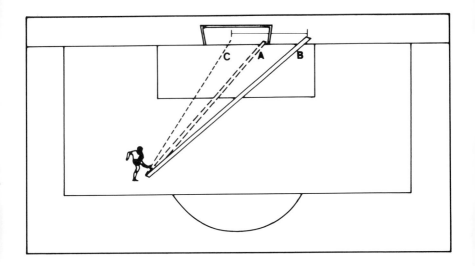

Give yourself margin for error. Here, the striker has aimed a shot just inside the right post (A) but, with no margin for error, it has gone well wide (B). To get the ball into that right post spot the next time, it would be better to aim more to the centre of goal (C).

The one distinct lesson that applies to all varieties of shooting — even volleying — is to keep your knee over the ball and your head down, so that you look at the ground after the ball has been struck and, indeed, until the follow-through has been completed.

Often, if you aim your shot at the near post, the ball goes in at the far post, and if you aim at the far post the ball goes wide! If this happens, then it is worth re-aligning your aiming spot. For example, you may have to aim at the centre of goal, to get the ball in at the far post. Believe it or not this is quite common among professionals.

It's the same with golf pros. Often a top golfer will have a natural bend to his driving shot (known as a "fade" or "draw") and have to play his shot accordingly. Goalscorers, like golfers, should always allow for the possible imperfection of their shots.

But first you must learn to shoot correctly in different situations.

There are five basic ways to strike at goal.

1. the straightforward drive
2. with the inside of the foot
3. with the outside of the foot
4. the volley
5. the chip.

The Straightforward Drive

A footballer's ability to master the straight drive is often frustrated by his desire to take the skin off the ball! Although the shot may look hard-hit, power is not achieved by brute strength.

A shot fired smoothly and properly timed, with the head and knee well over the ball, will automatically gain great speed.

Similarly, you do not require a huge backswing. Many of the most powerful strikers of the ball I have played with or against, seemed to hardly raise their leg at all.

Leeds's Peter Lorimer is a prime example. He had arguably the hardest shot in the League off an incredibly short backswing. Stewart Barrowclough, a team-mate of mine at Newcastle, also achieved great power with this method.

To practice the straightforward drive, begin with a still ball. Concentrate on getting the standing foot or ankle square to it, with the toe pointing directly along the line you wish to shoot.

Your standing leg will automatically bend slightly, reducing any possible tenseness of the body, and making your shooting action smooth — as long as you aim for accuracy, not power.

Then just bring your striking foot through to connect with the centre of the ball, while keeping your head well over, or past, the point of impact. At the point of contact, the toe of your striking foot should be pointing downwards.

41

Use your arms as a balance, to prevent unstableness, and continue looking at where the ball was. Your follow-through will bring your head up naturally. Many players have a natural lean to the side, away from the ball. That's fine, as long as the lean isn't backwards, because it is important to be comfortable and relaxed.

Aim being the all-important factor, it is useful to practice shooting 15 yards from a wall, and seeing how many times out of 20 you can hit a particular low target. Don't set an unrealistic target, like the proverbial sixpence. If it's a brick wall, draw a post and aim for a group of bricks representing the bottom corner of goal.

You may find that in your efforts to keep the ball down, you scuff the ground with your striking foot — don't worry! (Unless, of course, you've got your best shoes on!). That is not as much of a problem as sky-ing the ball. Simply work hard until you perfect a shot with a trajectory that keeps fairly low to the ground.

Then, remembering the goal is only eight feet high, raise the shot by *slightly* changing the angle of foot and body.

From there, move on to shooting at various angles. Start with the centre of the "D" on the edge of the penalty area seeking entry near a post or stanchion. Change to the opposite post or stanchion, then vary your shooting positions round the "D".

Having covered every possible angle of shot and entry, you can progress to shooting at goal with a goalkeeper and a moving ball.

Get a partner to roll a ball in, perhaps with an uneven bounce, and fire a shot, ensuring that your knee remains over the ball. This may seem as if you are firing into the ground, but the momentum of your follow-through will always raise the shot slightly.

Then, move on to a much harder exercise — hitting a ball directed at you from the dead-ball line. In this case, don't worry so much about hitting the corners of the goal, just make sure the ball goes inside the framework of posts and bar!

This is a difficult shot to accomplish, because it is struck towards goal at a right angle to its original direction.

Here, pay great attention to timing. It is important that your standing foot is well-positioned. The tendency is to lean into the line along which the ball has come — but that doesn't help accuracy!

Another difficult shooting situation arises when someone behind hits a ball for you to run onto. A common fault is to strike the ball when it is too far away, but this can be avoided by placing the standing foot past the ball, so that by the time you make contact, the ball lies square with it.

Every footballer has a "favourite" foot with which he is stronger and prefers to shoot and, although this should be perfected, never completely neglect your weaker limb!

Any defender will tell you that a totally one-footed player is the easiest to mark. If you have a strong left foot, but can also pack a punch with the right, then the centre-half is never certain on which side he is going to be attacked.

I recall playing for Newcastle against Hendon in the FA Cup Third Round in 1973. As I was running through, with the centre-half backing away, his covering team-mate shouted: "Force him onto his right foot!"

My marker did, and I scored from 25 yards. The next time, the centre half was told: "Get him on his left!" and I hit the bar.

By the third time, even I was awaiting the advice, and the order came loud and clear: "Make him head it!" That time I did lose the ball — laughing!

43

Chasing, and hitting, a forward pass. Before making contact, ensure that the standing foot is ahead of the ball.

44

Often you will have to take a defender on before shooting, as I did in that case, and it is sometimes best to just move the ball slightly wide of him — rather than try to actually go past him — before letting fly. That way you create space around your marker, and put the goalkeeper out of position.

The last situation in which the straightforward drive is of particular value is when performing the half-volley. Get a partner to throw the ball onto your chest, bring it down and strike in the normal fashion. Remember, though, that chest control invariably leaves you leaning backwards, so make sure you recover enough to get your head and knee over the ball.

When you're bearing down on goal, with a defender immediately in front of you, just concentrate on changing your shooting angle by a couple of feet rather than attempting to dribble around him.

Inside of the Foot

A player will often find that, when a cross comes in, the original passer has put some form of spin on the ball in an attempt to elude the defence.

Only when the straightforward drive has been perfected can a goalscorer learn to use that spin, by striking with the inside, or the outside, of the foot.

45

The curling shot with the inside of the foot.

Shooting with the inside of the foot is perhaps the easiest of the two tasks, because it is usually little more than a pass with extra power or swerve.

To begin with, any ball struck with the inside of the foot is almost guaranteed to curve, because one is invariably striking across it rather than through it.

A shot utilising the inside of the foot, and connecting across the face of the ball, is most effective 10-15 yards out from goal, but can be used at even closer range for a greater degree of accuracy if, for instance, the goalkeeper has advanced and shown a little too much of one side of the goal.

The natural swerve will take the ball wider than a straightforward shot, giving the keeper less chance of making a save.

It is also, perhaps the only form of shooting acceptable when one is leaning backwards! The reason is that it is unlikely height will be achieved with the inside of the foot.

Outside of the Foot

A "banana" shot with the outside of the foot.

Although similar in effect, shooting with the outside of the foot is a far harder technique to perfect.

Accuracy is most difficult. You are not permitted to close your foot around the ball — as you are when shooting with the inside — and the line that your foot will take is often completely opposite to the one in which the ball will go.

However, when successfully executed, it can cause goalkeepers and defenders all sorts of problems. Excessive curl will be achieved, enabling you to bend balls around defensive walls — very useful for free-kicks — and leave the 'keeper totally out of position.

It is also very hard to perform leaning over the ball, but make sure your knee is not too far back or you will sky the shot horrifically.

The best practice is always done with a motionless ball, experimenting with your angle of shot. It is very difficult to have overall control of your effort unless your positioning is perfect.

47

When discussing the volley, I can't stress enough the importance of getting over the ball, as demonstrated in the two top photographs above. Look at the difference between these photos and the one below, in which I am doing everything wrong.

If ever in doubt about how this shot should be carried out, the men to watch are Glenn Hoddle, Chris Waddle (Tottenham) and Kevin Sheedy (Everton)

The Volley

Volleying is the most difficult of all footballing skills to accomplish, and the percentage of players — even at international level — who have been able to master it is exceedingly low.

The simple explanation for this is that many just cannot break their everyday

kicking habits. To volley correctly means breaking every rule in the book!

Ask 100 junior footballers where they should connect on the ball when volleying, and 90 per cent will say the centre or just below.

They are very wrong. Striking the underneath of a ball in mid-air forces it only one way — upwards — so contact should be made as high on the ball as possible, ideally to the extent of almost attempting to force it into the ground.

If you fail to connect high enough you still have a margin of error and, even if the ball

Another volleying sequence, this time reiterating my favourite football philosophy. Yes, you've got it – GET IT, TURN, SHOOT! Here again, I've made contact as high on the ball as possible, thus ensuring that the shot is kept reasonably low.

Volleying a low ball ...

doesn't hit the floor, its trajectory should still be below eight feet.

The best way to practice this is to ask a partner to hold the ball with his palms underneath, while you constantly turn your leg over the ball to strike it into the ground.

From there you move on to doing that when the ball is being thrown at you.

When volleying a ball coming from the side, at waist height, the knees should be slightly crooked, pointing towards the ground. Thus, the leg moves in an arc motion, and the foot meets the ball at the top of that arc.

If you make contact on the upwards arc you will sky it; on the downward arc, and it will skid off the top of your foot.

The ball that arrives lower — for instance,

The overhead kick, arguably the most spectacular shot in the game. Even with this difficult technique, it's essential to make contact at the top of the ball.

below the thigh or knee — should be allowed to pass your standing leg and be struck on the downswing, getting the knee and the foot well over, and making contact slightly above the centre of the ball. The main thing is not to strike too early.

Having mastered the volley as a straightforward drive, you can progress to volleying with the inside or outside of the foot, to gain extra swerve.

If you apply the basic technique mentioned earlier, you shouldn't go far wrong, but don't expect instant success. Volleying with the inside of the foot, particularly, is extremely difficult as the shooting movement is unnatural.

On occasions you will be forced to volley without the bonus of a standing foot — a flamboyant action, most commonly referred to as the scissor or bicycle kick.

This is basically a walking motion in midair. You should be parallel to the goal and your kicking foot should move from backwards to forwards, your balancing foot from forwards to backwards. It is imperative that

51

the striking position is high — just below the top of the ball.

Another reason for always striking at the top of the ball is that, as the ball is in mid-air, the opposing defence and goalkeeper will be anticipating a high or rising shot.

Immense power can be obtained from volleying, but it still does not require a huge backswing from the striking leg. Again, accuracy is the most important factor.

The only time you should volley from underneath a ball is when performing the volley-lob.

In this case, the ball is often on its downward arc, with an opponent approaching. The ball will frequently be too high to shoot with a driving motion, and travelling too slowly to wait until it is right to do so. Therefore, you have only one course of action — the lob.

This should have enough height to ensure the goalkeeper cannot reach it, but not so much that it flies over the crossbar.

The kicking motion should involve a very delicate pulling of the knee towards the chin, with the foot on a downward angle into the floor.

As well as sending the ball up, this will create a topspin which should make the ball dip.

It is also necessary that, having lobbed the keeper, you should maintain your run towards goal. Should the ball rebound from the woodwork or be cleared from the line, you will then be well positioned for an easy tap-in. *Never* take for granted that you've scored or missed until the referee's whistle blows to signal either a goal scored or the ball is out of play.

*The volley-lob ... It
requires a delicate touch,
and is the only form of
volleying where you must
strike underneath the ball.*

The Chip

Chipping the ball — usually to capitalise on a goalkeeper who is too far from his line — is very difficult to master with a ball moving at speed.

With a still ball, however, it is relatively simple, although problems may occur maintaining a consistent degree of accuracy.

A chip needs to gain early height, so the foot needs to dig under the surface of the ball, without stubbing, taking a small divot. In many cases you will gently strike the surface before the ball, but this should not be a problem if you follow-through, creating a natural, upward, arc.

It is possible to chip without a follow-through but this should not be attempted until the more run-of-the-mill method has been perfected.

Position a number of balls outside the

penalty area, and see how many times you can hit the bar. I must stress that you mustn't get too despondent if everything doesn't fall into place at once. Consistently accurate chipping requires a lot of effort.

A rather more delicate skill is the curled chip, mastered by a mere handful of professionals. Here, the foot goes under and across the ball, swinging at an angle of 45 degrees, and causing it to rise in the air with swerve and spin.

This can be practiced with either the inside or outside of the foot — and becomes progressively harder the faster the ball is moving!

It is easier to chip a ball coming towards you, as it should gain a natural backspin.

The ball moving away is a different proposition and should only be attempted if *you* are moving faster than *it* is.

The curled chip with the inside of the foot.

In this instance, catch it up, position your standing foot past the ball and make contact as the ball arrives square to your standing ankle.

The most useful practice is to position a partner 25 yards away, and see how many times you can chip accurately to his feet, chest or thigh.

There is one further version of the chip, which is referred to as "The Dink". This is a shot, hit with pace, but using the chipping motion and implemented when the goalkeeper has spread himself low in an effort to stop a shot.

The "Dink" is performed by going through with a shooting motion, but flattening the foot to slip under the ball with enough power to reach the net at a height of 4-5 feet. There should be no follow-through at all.

The perfect "dink" should also dip as it reaches the line, and the technique required is very delicate.

When the chip "dink" or volley-lob cannot be performed in a one-on-one situation (you versus the goalkeeper, or the goalkeeper and one defender) your only option is to try a straight shot.

As I mentioned earlier, the best way is to dummy to shoot, then move the ball slightly to one side. This will cause the defender to attempt to block the dummied shot, balancing and positioning himself wrongly for the real one.

By moving the ball to one side by a couple of feet, you have now left the goalkeeper out of place. Remember, everyone on the field moves in relation to the angle of ball to goal. By moving the ball even a foot, you have left your opponents a step out of position at least.

Having done this, you must shoot instantly. Never allow the keeper to re-position, or the defender time to intercept.

Often, this action is performed while on the run, so it is vital that you learn to shoot in your stride.

As well as pushing the ball slightly wide, you have to lean into the defender so that he's not perfectly balanced. If he tries to slide across, he is liable to bring you down for a foul or penalty.

Now there's an interesting subject ... penalties. By blowing his whistle and pointing to the spot, a referee can subject a player to more instant pressure than he is likely to face in the entire match.

The opposition and their crowd begin barracking, the goalkeeper gets up to all sorts of tricks, your players cast eyes heavenwards in silent prayer and you are left with a lump in your throat and the feeling that all the world is against you!

The "Dink" – the only shot where there is no follow-through.

57

There is no simple answer to the question: how do you take a penalty? Most either sidefoot or drive, but you should pick whichever way feels most comfortable.

If you place the ball by sidefooting, your power of shot doesn't have to be as great and, if you blast it, you don't have to worry as much about positioning.

Many aim for the upper part of the goal — above four feet — and the softer your shot, the nearer you will need to be to the woodwork.

If you are opting for a straight drive always attempt to curl the ball away from the keeper, choosing a target area somewhere near the stanchion.

If you are left-footed aim for his left, if you are right-footed aim to his right, and the curl will be achieved naturally.

The most common fault when side-footing is leaning back, getting too much under the ball and hitting it over the bar.

The run-up is very important, and the shorter the better. Three - five yards should be ample, because the more steps you take, the more time — and signs — you give the goalkeeper to anticipate the destination of your shot. Above all, having begun your run, never change your mind about where you are placing your effort.

Keep your head down, and give yourself a solid, standing leg.

As ever, the biggest demand should be for accuracy. Organise penalty competitions with your friends and see who can hit two or three targets the most times. Always practice with more than one target, so your penalties don't become *too* predictable.

Probably the finest spot-kickers of the modern era have been Phil Neal and Bryan "Pop" Robson.

Both were able to hit to either side, and

rarely gave any indication of their intentions. Sidefooting with curl, they would appear to shape to knock the ball to one corner and then, at the last moment, change the angle of their foot and fire it to the other!

I scored and missed a number of penalties.

I particularly remember my penalty on my home debut for Newcastle against Liverpool, when we were trailing 0-1.

I struck the ball with the side of my left-foot and it flew into the top left-hand corner of the net. It missed the post and bar by inches, and afterwards, everyone came up to me with congratulations. They said what a fine penalty it was, and that few people could have managed such precision.

I didn't have the heart to tell them I had aimed for the bottom corner!

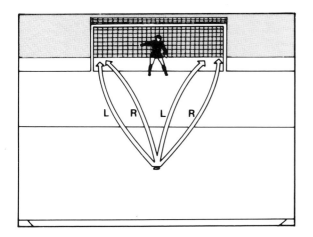

How to put goalkeepers on the spot!

4 · Heading

The way a striker heads a ball bears no resemblance to, say, a centre-half's method of heading. The centre-half is looking for distance and needs height, whereas accuracy and keeping the ball down (like volleying) are the main aims of the centre-forward.

Invariably, you will be off-balance, pushed and shoved, and rarely will you be allowed space for a clear effort at goal.

Fists will be flying and you run the risk of being clattered by the goalkeeper, so heading, once again, calls for immense bravery.

Very few strikers are successful without the ability to head the ball. Bryan "Pop" Robson was one, and Bobby Charlton another — both closed their eyes before jumping — but in general, the attitude seems to be: "I may get hit on the head a few times, but my goal will be in the record books forever, and a split eye soon heals."

A common misconception is that you have to be tall to be an aerial threat. This is not true as long as you have the ability to get in front of your marker.

The finest headers of the ball I have seen were Matt Tees, of Grimsby, Charlton and Luton, and Ron Davies of Chester, Luton, Norwich, Southampton, Portsmouth, Man-

chester United, Millwall and Wales. Both are remembered as being over 6 foot, when in fact they were little more than 5.10.

But they had great spring in their jump, great positional sense and timing. So did such little men as Kevin Keegan, Lou Macari of Manchester United and Scotland and Cliff Jones of Tottenham and Wales.

Big men don't necessarily make good headers of the ball, because they think height is enough and don't take such vital ingredients as the correct technique and positioning seriously.

Of the six-footers, perhaps Tony Hateley — Mark's father — and John Toshack were the finest. They both got the basics right, and put a lot of power into their headers.

It's not just in shooting that you need a good follow-through but heading, too. You arch your back and then punch into the ball, like a bow string after releasing an arrow.

Use your shoulders and arms to get across your marker ...

To go through the heading action, it is best to start at the ground floor and work up, beginning with the feet!

Everyone has a favourite shooting foot, and the same applies to a jumping foot. Watch anyone who achieves height with his jump and you will see that, just before his pushing foot goes into action, his other leg begins to rise to lift the body. Then the force comes from the jumping foot.

The next step is to move back at the waist, getting greater leverage into your movement into the ball, than you would if merely heading from the neck.

Denis Law was the best exponent of this and, for a little man, got extreme power when he did connect. His jump would be backwards and then his entire upper torso would "punch" into the ball.

Your arms should be squarely out, but crooked at the elbow with your fists jutting

... and always head the ball down.

forward. This prevents players barging you out of the way, and "buys" you more space to get your header in.

Your aim should always be to get your arm above that of your marker. This way, you will get higher in the air and, if he pushes against you, you can use him as a balance, even to the extent of helping yourself onto the ball.

Now we get to the actual process of putting head to ball; always try to get your eye-line level with its centre or just below. Aim at the general target of the goal, as opposed to a specific spot — it is very rare that you will have time to be more precise.

In most circumstances head downwards, as the defence and goalkeeper will all be moving up, and you will catch them on the hop. Also, it is very easy to head over the bar, so even if you don't head to the ground, the ball should at least stay below eight feet.

A header to the top right or left corner is very difficult to stop but generally, it should only be attempted if you have a "free" header — in other words, you are totally unmarked.

Invariably, though, you will be under pressure from a defender, so the aim of all positioning for high crosses and lofted through balls should be to get across him.

63

Most centre-halves are big men and thus quite slow, and you can use your pace to nip in front. He might only be six inches away, but you can still appear to outjump him because, while you are in mid-air, he has yet to get off the ground!

The centre-half might even think a shorter man poses no problem, and allow you plenty of space. Never waste it — if you are a small forward, work doubly hard on your heading so that, when a rare chance presents itself, you can take full advantage.

To get across your marker, the run must always be made late, from outside the box or area. How often do you see a fine cross sail over everyone's heads because they didn't have the patience to time their run in accordance with the cross?

So always move into the path of the cross, don't backtrack to receive it. You won't be able to run as fast, nor sum up the goalmouth situation as well.

In certain cases, you should run diagonally away from the ball, to return in a chevron shape for your attack on goal.

This should occur a mere two seconds before the ball arrives, giving you a good angle on goal and the option of either making a loop to come in at the far post, or a flat sprint in the direction of the near post.

You have to take a gamble about where the ball is going to land and then — go! It is pointless standing around waiting for it to drop on your head, because it never will.

Although it is extremely difficult to aim for a specific target when heading, certain circumstances dictate, for instance, one half of the goal as the best spot.

A good example would be the cross that falls outside the far post. The goalkeeper will instinctively cover the nearest post to you, and it is best to head across him so that (a) the

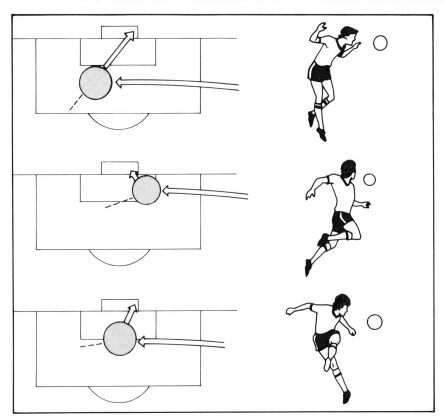

ball might creep in the uncovered part of goal or (b) it will run parallel to the line, thus giving a team-mate a simple chance.

If you meet the ball at the centre of goal, it is common that you will be running in on an angle, and it's best to aim the ball back on its line. It is probable that the goalkeeper will be following the path of the ball, and will suddenly have to change direction.

If you are standing at the near post and the cross is driven in, it is likely that the keeper will be in close attention and you will have little or no room for the flicked header goalwards.

Then you have to forget all selfish motives, and head back across goal for a colleague to complete the move.

The only time you are likely to have any joy from a near post header is from a corner kick. Most goalkeepers stand at the far post and,

Three different types of goalscoring headers. The punch header is generally used for a cross to the far post, the glancing header for a cross to the near post. As for a cross to the centre of the goal, the technique required to put the ball in the net can best be described as a subtle combination of the other two!

with a subtle glance, you might just squeeze the ball past the covering centre-back.

There is only one exception to the rules about heading downwards, or across the face of goal, and this is usually the upshot of bad goalkeeping.

On occasions, the 'keeper, in attempting to catch a cross, will commit himself before realising interception is impossible. While that's happening, you should already be looking out the corner of your eye, and making split-second decisions about distances, angles and positioning.

When the ball arrives, you should get your head underneath to loop it over the goalkeeper's head, and under the bar.

The most simple and obvious form of practice is to get a winger out wide and ask him to kick balls in for you at various heights, angles and distances to goal.

Practice running in to head a ball — never stand still — and changing direction at the last moment. Get to know the sort of balls a certain team-mate will produce, so that you are always ready for his crosses. By knowing what to expect, you can gain an extra foot on your marker.

Another useful practice — and one used by most football clubs — is to have a ball hanging on a rope and suspended from the roof of the gymnasium.

By heading the ball at different heights, a player can quickly get his timing right.

As for diving headers, your momentum is usually enough to power the ball over the line, but if you have enough time, a small flick of the head can place the ball to one particular corner.

But the main requirement is bravery. Not many players will stick their heads among the flying boots in a crowded six yard area or penalty box.

5 · Losing your Marker

There are two basic ways of defending — zonal marking and man-for-man.

The zonal system involves each defender occupying an area on the pitch, marking any forward who moves into it. If the forward then runs out of that zone, he is passed on to the next defender.

Man-for-man is as simple as it sounds. Every defender is allotted a forward to mark, and he stays with him whatever.

Many sides play a mixture of both systems, but I have yet to come across a completely different third method.

Therefore, if I deal with each in turn, I will have covered almost every back four tactic.

The Zonal System

Even in the zonal system, your marker will frequently adopt the man-for-man method, *but only within the boundaries of his certain area.* Also, because zonal marking is not so strictly regimented, you will probably be given more freedom when the ball is not close to you.

Perhaps the easiest way to exploit the zonal system in this situation, is to join forces with your forward partner, and play two against one.

This will give you the few seconds needed to organise yourself for an attack on goal and, by pulling the defender away from his zone, will leave a hole through the back-line for a team-mate to go into.

The forward can also create space in which to work by spinning off the centre-half and making runs wide, behind the full-back.

The centre-half will be wary of moving outside his area which, again, will create space for your partner to exploit — and unbalance the opposing back four line.

But the only way to discover your marker's limitations, what he will and will not do, is to come off him and experiment.

I often found that my marker was far happier dropping back than going forward. If he won't follow you deep, it will give you space to collect the ball, turn and run at him.

Having done this a number of times, the centre-half will probably begin to follow you upfield, leaving a space behind for your forward partner or a midfielder to exploit.

As soon as defenders solve one problem, give them another. Never let them feel relaxed.

That is why it is always worth spending 10-15 minutes at the start of each game, just probing a defence's weaknesses.

What will they do? What won't they do? Where will they "travel"? Where won't they "travel"?

Quite simply, any forward who is content to just stand still and be marked, thinking he'll hold the defender off when the ball arrives, is wasting his — and everyone else's — time!

Once the centre-half sees you are happy to

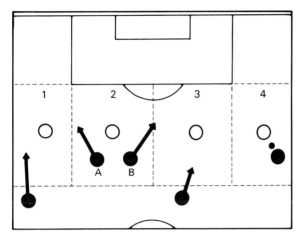

How to beat the zonal marking system – by creating two-against-one situations. In each case, the support of your midfield team-mates is essential.

Top, the two strikers, A and B, are both in one central defender's zone. The defenders in zones 1 and 3 are caught in two minds about covering the strikers' runs because midfielders are moving into their areas too.

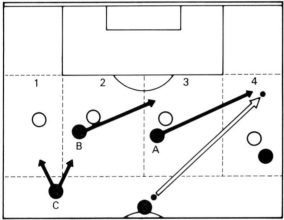

Middle, the ball is hit into the space beyond the outside right and his marker, for striker A to run onto, and striker B runs into zone 3 in support. Normally, the latter's marker would be expected to go with him – but, here again, note the problems caused by the run of a midfielder (C).

Bottom, the advantages of a midfielder going forward with the ball. Note, too, the "shape" of striker A's run to first draw the defender away, and then get the midfielder's pass without being caught offside.

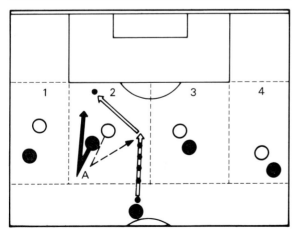

stand still, he will become confident, and that must *never* be allowed to happen. At all times make him work, make him think. Look lively, look confident, look glad to be playing.

Once he sees that, he'll start worrying. He'll think: "What's he looking so pleased about? What does he know that I don't? What am I doing wrong?"

And that's half of your work done!

Man-For-Man Marking

Many of the tips to combat man-for-man marking, are also applicable in the zonal situation.

Man-for-man marking is a battle of wits between you and your marker and, again, your primary objective is to disturb his thinking and performance.

The defender will not stand directly behind you, but a little to one side, in between you and the goal. This is an attempt to force you wide, away from your target, but has the side effect of enabling you to be in front and get the ball.

Therefore you must have an understanding with your fellow players, demanding that they pass the ball to your "freer" foot (the foot

By turning away from your marker (A), not into him (B), you keep your body between him and the ball, and he has to cover considerably more ground to dispossess you.

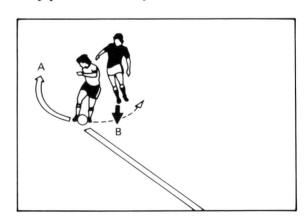

70

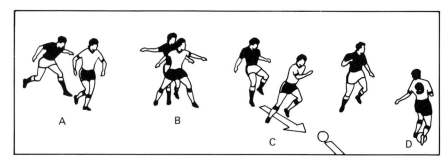

further from the defender), giving you the opportunity to run wide and cut back in.

Your initial turn must always be away, otherwise your marker will cut the ball off by nipping in front. To prevent this, just before the ball is to be played, push back and slightly bump into him, using his weight as a springboard for your acceleration. He is now on his heels, you on your toes and shaping to receive the ball.

Once you have possession you can turn and run at him at speed.

Centre-forwards should grasp every opportunity to take their markers on. Always run at pace. Threaten to go either way and he'll be caught on his heels, in two minds about your direction. Most defenders are slow men and,

Getting away from your marker.

Top, the striker comes off his opponent (A), suddenly stops, causing his opponent to bump into him (B). That creates the impetus for the striker to sprint forward again (C) and turn with the ball before the defender can get back to him (D).

Bottom, being tightly marked doesn't always mean you getting long balls "over the top" (A). By coming off your marker as shown ((B) and (C)) you are now in a good position to have the ball played to your left, facing the opposing goal.

although they may try to force you wide, they won't get half the chance if you have built up enough speed.

You might be unlucky and pick on a defender with a bit of pace and good in the tackle — but you'll never know until you try!

Similarly, if the defender is pushing tight on you from the back, you can still turn and, if you are quick enough, he might even fall forward as your weight disappears. That, also, might not work — but remember you are licenced to lose the ball in an attempt to score goals.

Your job is to create a scoring chance from the proverbial "nothing", and you will only do that by experimenting. The art of the goal-scorer is to leave a crowd gasping: "Now, how the hell did he do that?"

The nearer you get to the area, the tighter man-for-man marking will be employed, and goals can be created by your ability to exploit weaknesses in fractions of seconds.

The first manoeuvre to practice is "checking". Quite simply, take one step in one direction, then dart off in the other. If the marker is close, you may have left him cold by a foot or two. Next time, check the opposite way.

Check one step forward, then suddenly take off and run around the back. If your midfielder has the foresight to realise your intentions, he will have played a long ball over the centre-half's head, and you could be in a yard of space, running on goal.

That is why it is all-important to build your pace up to its ultimate level — the quicker you are, the more success you will have when "checking". And the harder you'll be to catch when running on goal.

If absolutely nothing is going right, you've lost every ball, the centre-half's wearing a silly big, confident grin, try standing still.

Remain rooted to a spot and see what the centre-half does. He might stand with you, in which case you'll have to think again, or he might drift away, giving you a bit of space.

Even if he stands with you, all is not necessarily lost. You can suddenly make a run and hope your midfielders see it before your marker does.

Never just amble away from the centre-half, because you'll make yourself very easy to mark. Everything you do should be bright and nippy. nothing is more off-putting than a centre-forward with quick, little steps who looks as if he really wants the ball, and is ready to attack the defence.

A small percentage of teams, in addition to operating one of the two conventional marking systems, will also play an offside trap, especially those sides who favour the zonal method.

I must make the point that teams can only play an "offside trap" if the opposing forwards are foolhardy or impatient enough to make their runs too early.

If your opponents are known to use the trap, then you must be doubly aware of the position of their defenders. It is very easy for

This is what the pros mean when they talk of "checking". I suppose a better description would be "Check Mate"!

Before the ball has been hit to him, the striker has sprinted two or three yards to one side (taking his marker with him), knowing full well that the ball will be played to the spot he has left. Suddenly, he stops, spins back ... and away he goes.

73

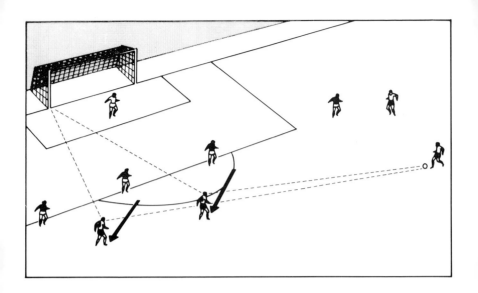

How to beat the offside trap (1). Move out, with the defenders ... move out backwards, and away from the ball as well as the goal, to give yourself the best angle of vision possible (dotted line).

them to anticipate a through-ball and, seconds before it is played, nip sharply forward leaving you 3-4 yards offside.

I am frequently amazed that forwards are caught offside in positions that are not conducive to goalscoring anyway!

If you can see that the defenders are ready to step up, dart back, away from them, so that you can make your run for the through ball from a deeper, and on-side, position.

It is vital to have a good understanding with your co-striker. It is pointless running yourself into the ground in an attempt to remain on-side, if he wanders about half-asleep behind the defensive line.

Always work in opposite directions — with only one making the run for goal — but make sure you are well aware of each other's movements.

As I mentioned in an earlier chapter, when an offside trap is being implemented, it is also important that the winger crosses first time. If he shapes to cross, and then gives the ball an extra-touch, it is a sure sign that you will be caught in no-man's land.

Always run diagonally, never straight at

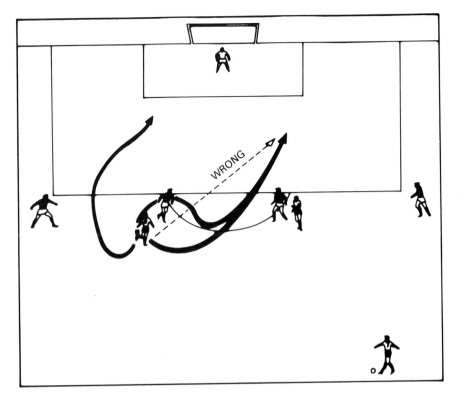

How to beat the offside trap (2). Make curving runs – never run in a straight line.

goal. Otherwise, the defence will simply step up, and you will give away a free-kick.

Curved runs will line you up for the through-pass, *and* keep you onside. Discovering this, the defence might begin to drop off. Then it is vital that the ball is played to your feet, not to the hole that the centre-half has filled.

Until now, I have mostly dealt with losing your marker 30-40 yards from goal. A different set of rules apply in and around the penalty area.

For instance, "space" takes on a totally different meaning in that part of the field. If you can get six inches away from your marker, enough to get a shot in — that's "space". "Time", too, is different, and we begin dealing, not with seconds, but with fractions of seconds, because that's all it takes to score a goal.

75

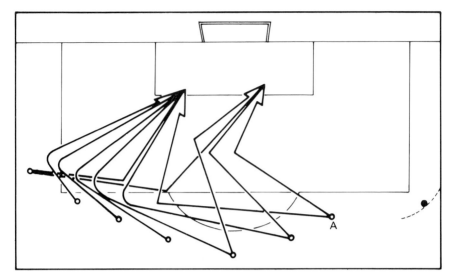

How to beat the offside trap (3). The shape of these near and far post runs, from six different positions around the penalty area, are not just meant to keep the linesman's flag down. Let's take the man nearest the ball (A). If you were to draw a line from him to the near post, and get him to run on that line for the cross, he will be easy to mark, and won't be able to see the ball until the last moment. Hence the need for the sort of run I have outlined. It also gives him greater scope to "lose" his marker.

You'll be dealing with a massed defence, and your first requirement should be that your fellow players do not crowd your space, by getting in the box too early and hanging around.

It is better to play two against three, than six against six. You'll have to say: "If you want to come in, then arrive late for the knock-downs, and leave the first ball for me."

Bryan Robson, at Manchester United, is the perfect example of a midfielder who realises the needs of his forwards in and around the box. His timing and patience is impeccable and, while never cluttering the box, he scores a tremendous amount of goals.

Having sorted out the positioning of yourself and your team-mates, you can begin considering losing your marker in potential goalscoring situations.

When he has a defender close behind, a striker's first-time shot on the turn will often leave the goalkeeper unsighted.

The centre-half who stands off can be beaten by controlling the ball, perhaps two yards away from your body and then firing a shot on the turn.

In both cases, you shouldn't need to aim,

because a good striker will already know where the goal is.

This is easily done by constantly assessing your position in relation to the posts and pitch markings. They never change, so by being aware of your angle to them, you should know your distance and position from goal.

Once you appreciate that, getting a shot in becomes easier, because you utilise space and can get away from your marker without taking up an impossible angle.

Keep checking, however near you may be to goal.

If things are getting a bit cramped in the box, don't be frightened to run out, to get a better look at the situation. You then have the perfect viewpoint to make a better run back in.

Always check or bend your runs — three yards to the left, three to the right — because the more times you change direction, the harder you become to mark. Straight runs are the easiest to counter.

Don't be worried about pushing into the centre-half. If you can get him prodding you, that's fine. Listen for his feet, his studs and, in time, you'll be able to tell whether he's on his toes or his heels.

Even playing at Wembley, in front of 100,000 screaming fans, I could always hear a clodhopping centre-half approaching!

6 · The Six-Yard Box

I have so far talked of the opposing half in general, everywhere bar the smallest area that it holds, the six-yard box.

Here, the goalscorer lives by a different set of rules.

Invariably, you'll be working among a lot of players — defenders especially — frantically throwing themselves about. And whilst all around are losing their heads, this is the one area in which the goalscorer *must* remain ice cool.

Brian Clough, who scored 251 goals in 274 games for Middlesbrough and Sunderland, has said that it only takes a fraction of a second to get a goal. That is why the forward in the six-yard box must be ever alert.

Your thinking must be totally different to that of everyone else. A defender is waiting to clear with head or feet, tackle or simply close down; a goalkeeper is ready for a save to the left or right, up or down, backward or forward, to catch the ball or punch it. All these possibilities pass through his mind. But you have just one option: scoring.

Already, through lack of choice, you have

the upper hand. It should be impossible for a forward to get caught in two minds inside the six-yard box. However you get the vital touch doesn't matter. Whatever part of the body prods the ball into that vast target — the goal — makes no difference.

You also have an advantage in a physical sense. The six-yard box is where defenders are most wary of fouling, for fear of giving away a penalty, and you should be prepared to knock them about to get that ever-elusive toe-poke! I'm not suggesting you should deliberately foul — but use the defenders as "buffers" to rebound off.

At no time stand still, be on your toes and take a risk.

Defenders have to be 100 per cent certain of clearing, while you have a greater margin of error. No forward can be expected to score every time, and it is simply a case of gambling, or anticipating, where the ball will go, and getting there first.

Although the six-yard box is strictly the domain of the goalkeeper, you should also lay claim to it as your patch, and impose stringent demands on your team-mates.

Basketball, too, has a small area surrounding the goal (or "basket"), known as "the key". Each player is allowed to spend no more than three seconds in the "key" at a time. Stay in for longer, and you give away a foul.

I told my colleagues to treat the six-yard box in the same way as the "key". "If you've been in there for more than three seconds and the ball hasn't arrived, get out, because you'll only eat up space for me."

Always try to stand in space and have your arms, hips and standing leg well positioned to ward off challenges if the ball arrives.

Probably the finest forward I have ever seen inside the six-yard box was West Germany's Gerd Muller.

79

He turned anticipation and simple awareness into an art form with his scruffy little
kicks, toe-pokes and deflections.

Everyone in the stand would think: "You
lucky so and so." Few realised that Muller
had worked just as hard for that one kick, as
the man who had avoided three tackles to get
the cross in.

Never give up looking for defensive mis-
takes. The law of averages says that you must
be right some of the time. To give you a
guideline — if you score from one out of
every five or six rebounds, you're a good
guesser.

I would estimate that a tenth of all a
striker's goals come from anticipating a
rebound in the six-yard area.

If you're ever in any doubt, watch old films
of Gerd Muller. He kept a defence thinking,
and if they ever stop thinking about you,
you're doing *something* wrong.

It is very rare that you'll be allowed the
time to control a ball in the six-yard box
before firing a shot, but when you do, you'll
invariably have to control and shoot with the
same foot.

Don't worry if you haven't achieved the
perfect strike. When you are just six yards
from goal — or nearer — any contact with the
ball is often all that is required to score.

Because there is such little space and time
inside the six-yard box, this skill has to be
practiced, practiced, practiced until it can be
achieved as quickly as possible.

If the ball is coming to you diagonally or
square, and it is impossible to hit first time,
attempt to control it back on its own path
and then strike.

Or, take the initial pace off the ball, but let it
run on, away from you and your marker, and
then make a strike as you spin around the
ball.

To shoot correctly inside the six-yard box, you must completely clear your mind of everything else.

Set your shooting sights high in and around the six yard box.

Whereas, from 20 yards, you should be aiming low, I have always told youngsters to aim for the roof of the net once inside the six-yard box.

No doubt most coaches will be horrified by this non-textbook suggestion, but there is a very good and simple explanation.

Defenders and goalkeepers will come at you low, and your shot has to be high enough to rise over their challenges.

Don't worry about placing your shot. Just get it within the general target with the minimum of fuss in the shortest possible time.

Don't take a long backswing and concentrate on propelling the ball quickly over a short distance.

You have to be on your toes and take a gamble where the pass or cross is going to go. It is very rare that you'll be blessed with a "good" ball in the six-yard box. You'll normally have to produce a volley or a toe-poke, due to the lack of space and time, and

81

obviously it is easier to aim for the roof of the net when presented with the former.

As time is of the essence, never look at the goal before shooting. This gives the defender and goalkeeper a fraction of a second to re-position.

Frankly, if you don't know where the goal is, what are you doing there?

Similarly, don't try to "place" a header, as you would if given more time.

The goal is eight feet high and eight yards wide and, as long as you get your head to the ball, you should be able to hit such a huge area.

Defenders and the goalkeeper will come flying at you, so keep your arms up and your elbows out, not just for protection, but as a barrier. By creating space in the usual way — running across your marker — you should get your head in first.

You're more likely to get kicked, punched, elbowed and clattered jumping for a ball in the six-yard box than anywhere else, but that is the supreme test of a goalscorer. Are you prepared to meet that challenge and be first?

Positioning and anticipation are all-important inside the six-yard box, and both aspects of the game need to be worked on.

It is vital to keep moving, because as you do, the angle to ball and goal changes and everyone has to re-position. But don't merely move for the sake of it. Everything you do should be with the ultimate objective of putting the ball in the net.

Also, a forward, like a goalkeeper, should perfect a crouch, because the smaller you are the more you are balanced due to a lower centre of gravity. The smaller and "squarer" you are, the quicker you will be, like a powerful cat ready to spring.

Having adopted the correct attitude and shape, you can begin to work on your

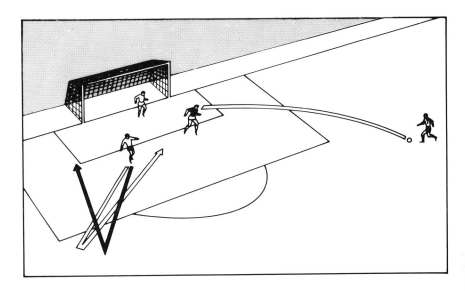

positioning and angles inside the box.

Remember the golden rule about an over-crowded area. When in doubt, backpeddle out to get a clearer view and then return on a new, hopefully better, angle.

The same applies when the ball is cleared. There is always a chance that a team-mate will gather it on the edge of the area, or 30 yards out, and set up another attack. You should move out on a diagonal line away from the goal, (whilst increasing your distance from the ball) ready to run back in a 'V'-shaped diagonal to fire at goal. If your team-mate does his job properly, the pass he knocks back into the area should dissect your line of approach to goal. It is then up to you to get your timing perfect to meet the ball.

Always run out backwards, never with your back to goal. Keep looking at the goal and over your shoulder, and stand slightly side-on so that the entire picture of team-mates, ball, defence, area and goal can be seen.

Moving out of the area to get a better view of it. This illustration, showing a ball being headed out and due to be knocked back in, is also another example of how to prevent being caught offside.

83

In this way, if you do get the ball at your feet, you can easily move forward while the defender will have to back-peddle. Also, unlike the defender, you will be totally aware of the task ahead.

Position yourself in anticipation of a possible rebound. Move backwards, away from the goal and the spot where you think the ball might land, so that when it happens, all you need are a couple of short forward steps to produce the finishing touch.

A great many clubs spend time in training practicing running backwards. Players will do a 100 yard sprint, 50 forwards, 50 backwards. Few players understand why, but you would be amazed at the amount of times you will be required to backpeddle in a match situation. Make sure you are fast going forwards, backwards and even sideways.

Although there is no substitute for match experience, your awareness in the six-yard box can be developed on the training field.

All you need is five willing helpers, and a goalkeeper. Now position the outfield men in a semi-circle around you, and get them to throw the ball anywhere in the six-yard box. Your job is to get on the end of their throw and turn it, with one touch, into the goal.

An extension of this is for them to kick the ball hard, with you having to deflect or divert it into the goal. These kicks should be made in quick succession, so that as you are rising from, say, a diving header you have to leap across the six-yard box to push one in with a toe. It keeps you alert and teaches you the subtle deflections and changes of angles that are essential to all top goalscorers.

Similarly, get them to stand in the middle of the 'D' and aim shots straight at you. With a little flick of your hips you can divert the shot, from the centre of goal, where the goalkeeper might be standing, to a corner.

Finally, the last, and most important lesson about operating in the six-yard box.

One of the hallmarks of a goalscorer is that when there's a hell of a scramble, with legs flying everywhere, and the ball finally trickles over the line, he's the one with his hand in the air first!

7 · Anticipation

What was it inside the mind of Jimmy Greaves that enabled him to see a goalscoring chance where another, equally skilled footballer saw nothing?

The answer: radar!

The man who has 20 chances and scores from 10 (a 50 per cent success rate) is not as valuable to a side as the man who sees 60 chances and converts 15 (a 25 per cent success rate). It is your *potential* to score goals that matters because, on a good day, most of your chances will go in.

If you don't see the chance, you won't score the goal.

Top snooker players are playing five shots ahead in their mind, and that is also the way of the goalscorer. He must be many moves ahead of what is happening on the field, because he has to gamble where the ball will finish up, and get there.

The word "gamble" is particularly applicable to my former profession.

Most goalscorers couldn't win money on a one-horse race, but nevertheless they are the supreme punters on the football field. They study form — that of their team-mates, their opponents and their own — make a judgement and stick by it.

I don't believe goalscorers are merely "lucky". Luck invariably runs out, yet Jimmy Greaves's never did.

People also tell me that goalscorers are born and not made. I disagree. They *can* be created, as long as they have the abilities we have mentioned, complemented by the right attitude.

The majority of footballers go out to please the crowd, their team-mates, their manager, coach, board of directors and the media. The goalscorer goes out to please no-one but himself, and makes a lot of enemies in the process.

You have to make a study of everyone you play with, everyone you play against, and have an implicit understanding of what makes them tick, what they are thinking, their personalities, their strengths and weaknesses.

A goalscorer would be left high and dry without colleagues to fetch and carry for him, and he must also know opponents to such a degree that, at any one time, he can take a picture in his mind, and decide on a course of action as a result of that picture.

And that is on top of guessing the final destination of the ball!

The ability to do this is known as "the radar", and very few people — even within the game — understand it.

The radar is that picture in your mind that says: "The ball will finish *here*." Having done that you take a gamble on being right.

Over and above shooting, heading or control, the radar will get goals for you. Then obviously, the better you are at these basic skills the more you will be able to capitalise on it.

87

Simply, the radar decides who succeeds and who fails; who is in the right position and who is in the middle of the box when the ball sails over his head to the far post!

A goalscorer is the man who makes a run into an area with only a 100-1 chance of the ball arriving.

The worst feeling in the world is when you think: "Oh, this cross will be cut out, it's not worth bothering to make a run." Then the ball actually arrives and you aren't there.

You've got to chase 1,000 lost causes to score from one — but it's this sort of determination that grabs acclaim, headlines, huge transfer fees and the highest wages. When things aren't going right, though, it's the worst job in the world.

Most of the time you'll disregard the advice of your elders and betters. A coach will tell you to do something and you'll ignore him. In half of these instances, you won't even know why. It's just a feeling, an instinct, a premonition.

If you ever feel uncomfortable in a position on the field, you shouldn't be there. You might move to another spot 60 yards from goal, but if you feel comfortable, it must be the right one.

Never deliberate on anything but scoring. Forget the rest of the game — that is the job of your team-mates. Everything you do must be governed by one, simple, thought. "I will score a goal."

You'll be fuming when people misinterpret your runs, but must learn to curb such feelings and concentrate on creating the next chance.

For a goalscorer, there are only two forms of success:— (i) seeing a goal chance; (ii) converting it. You must defend your misses with the thought: "I may have missed that time, and I'll no doubt miss again; but

I'll continue missing until one gets in."

And when it does, never feel total satisfaction. Your strongest emotion must be a hunger for the second. And when the second goes in, a hunger for the third.

The only consolation when being in the wrong place at the wrong time, is that the only person who knows is you.

Only you will know the number of times you have run to the near post and the ball has been crossed to the far post. When the ball does come to the near post for you to hit a cracking goal, only you will know of the hard work put in before that. So don't expect anyone to acknowledge it!

A goalscorer has to be an optimist. Never fail to bother, and never think: "I can't do that." Always go out in the belief that you'll score a hat-trick.

While playing for Newcastle, shortly after recovering from a cartilage operation, I went five games without scoring — my longest "dry" spell — and a reporter asked for an interview after the fifth match.

"Well, Mal," he began, "you must be worried."

I didn't understand the question, and asked him to repeat it. He did so.

"I can't comprehend what you're saying," I replied. "The more games I go without scoring, the nearer I come to scoring a hat-trick. It's the law of averages. Of course I'm not worried."

"You're winding me up!" he said, switched off his tape recorder, and disappeared.

I truly didn't understand the question. As far as I was concerned, I would score a hat-trick in the next game. I never started a match feeling any other way. All goalscorers should have that belief — "I am unstoppable, I will score goals."

The strange thing was, I scored in the next

match, and didn't stop for 11 consecutive games!

The man who taught me not to worry if I missed, was dear old Jimmy Andrews, my coach at Luton.

I was playing for Luton against Birmingham at St. Andrews, and we were 0-1 down. I was clear through and looked certain to score; so certain, in fact, that the crowd were silent in anticipation. There was only one course of action open to defender Roger Hind — he pulled me down, and the referee awarded a penalty.

With the equaliser poised in the balance, the crowd began barracking. By the time I was ready to take the kick, the St. Andrews fans were whistling.

One thought was running through my mind: "I'll shut them up. I hope I don't miss. Please don't let me miss."

But it was a good penalty, hitting the net just inside a post. I was so relieved that, as it did so, I gave the crowd a "V"-sign.

After the match, Jimmy gave me the biggest talking to of my life!

"You're not a goalscorer, son!" he stormed. "You're still too worried about missing. Look, it doesn't matter whether you miss or score, get in and have a go! If you miss, you'll take stick — don't worry. If you score, you've had your say, and that should be it. Get on with scoring the next one."

He was right, of course.

If you watch the reaction of a striker after the ball has gone in, he'll celebrate, but usually for the crowd and his team-mates. The real satisfaction is inward. The feeling that it was all worth it.

And as you grow to understand your function, you'll grow to understand that of your team-mates and opponents. And finally, that of the radar.

Missing three and scoring one might not seem like a good average but, at the end of the season, if you have missed 400 and scored 110, it's better than having missed 40 and scored 19.

The highest scorer in the country this season will also no doubt be the best misser in the land!

But never be satisfied to miss because, although it is an inescapable part of the goalscorer's game, it is still failure.

Nobody has ever achieved perfection, and even if you've scored 100 goals from 100 chances there is no cause to be smug. Because there could have been a time when you didn't see a chance that would have made it 101!

It all comes down to "The radar" — but how can you develop it?

First, work incessantly on your shooting, control, heading and positioning and, when you are not on the field training, go home and think about your game. Then, when a chance does come up, you should be technically competent to put it away.

Also, look and learn. As a young player, I would watch as much "live" football as I could and study individuals. I would come out and hardly know the score, but I would be able to tell you every move, say, Jimmy Greaves made.

I would even watch defenders and goal-keepers if there was any likelihood that I would play against them.

But the most important thing was to watch my betters at other clubs, people like Greaves, and see how *they* went about the business of scoring goals.

One day after training at Luton, Jimmy Andrews said to me: "We've not got a match tonight, Mal," he said. "so I want you to go to West Ham."

"No can do, Jim," I replied, "I'm going to the pictures."

"You're going to West Ham," he said, "and you're going to study Geoff Hurst."

"Oh, come on Jim. I've got a date with Clint Eastwood at the Odeon at 8!"

"No you haven't. You're going to bloody West Ham, and you're watching Geoff Hurst!"

So, against my better judgement, and hardly relishing the journey from Bedfordshire to the East End of London, I set off to watch Hurst, whom I had only previously seen on TV.

Before I left, Jimmy told me: "You're quick and get in good positions, but you don't get into them enough. Watch Hurst, don't take your eyes off him."

It was a revelation. He opened my eyes to a particular aspect of my game which I was bad at. Previously, I wasn't mobile enough in the area. Hurst, though, never stopped repositioning and changing his angles. That 90 minutes in the stand made me a better player. It did more than Jimmy Andrews ever could, if he had worked on the training field with me for a whole week.

I can remember picking up a national newspaper one Saturday morning in mid-January, when the normal weekend fixture programme had been disrupted by bad weather.

A journalist had interviewed eight players who had a free Saturday, enquiring what they would be doing that afternoon.

I was stunned to find that only one of the eight, Manchester United's Gordon Strachan, had any intention of watching one of the few matches deemed playable — and even he was going to a game in the lower divisions.

This brought home to me just how lightly some professionals treat their careers, and the disregard they seem to have for improving themselves. It is so important to look and learn.

People often ask me what would I term a goalscoring chance? The only answer is, any situation where you have the remotest possibility of getting a shot on target.

Commentators talk of "half-chances" but, to me, there has never been such a thing.

How can one chance be half as good as another? If the man scored, it was a chance. Simple as that.

Chances are made by goalscorers, they don't appear from nowhere, and all are of equal importance, whether converted from 30 yards out, or three.

The biggest crime for any goalscorer is to disregard a potential shooting opportunity. The radar will tell you that every shot has equal possibilities.

So far, I have generally outlined what the radar is, and how, by studying your team-mates, your opponents and yourself you can acquire it. I worked hard at this aspect of my game, and here are some examples of how my knowledge of the men I played with and against helped me ...

Team-mates

TERRY HIBBITT, at Newcastle, would strike the ball without ever giving any indication of the direction the pass would go. Because he never looked up, the defenders never had an inkling.

But, by playing with Terry, I got to know the sort of ball he favoured and would run accordingly. It might have looked to all the world as if the pass would be short, but I would spin and run as he struck it, and most of the time it would be a 40-yarder. Thus I had gained 10 yards on a dumbstruck defence, left appealing for offside.

It took a season for that rapport to develop — but it happened.

JOHN TUDOR was my co-striker at Newcastle, and it needed a bit of kidology on my part before I could operate with him successfully. John was a far better player than me, technically, but inside was a frustrated coach trying to get out. Therefore, he would involve himself in every aspect of the game — and I was happy to encourage him to do that because he was taking on much of my responsibility in terms of build-up play!

I kept telling him what a great job he was doing. Thus, he was happy to take on virtually all of the "donkey work" ... and I was able to concentrate solely on scoring.

ALAN BALL, who I played with for Arsenal and England, was the best first-time passer in the game — we used to call him "Mr. One-Touch".

He would always play the ball to one side of the defender. Therefore, you could delude a defender by making him think the ball would come in on one foot, all the time knowing it would come in on the other.

He gave a lot of thought to his centre-forwards — a brilliant player, and a goal-scorer's dream.

TREVOR ROSS, a team-mate at Arsenal, had a cross which resembled most footballers' shots! If he was crossing from near the corner flag, the trajectory of the ball would only start to drop beyond the far post. Therefore, I would always make my approach run wider than normal, and attack the ball on a more acute angle.

Trevor Ross's crossing.

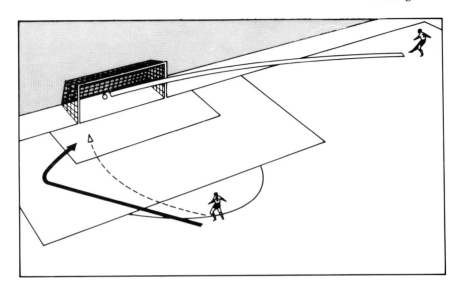

LIAM "CHIPPY" BRADY, whom I had the pleasure of playing with at Arsenal, taught me to expect the unexpected!

For instance, he would beat three or four players and get to the six-yard box to give himself the chance of an easy tap-in past the goalkeeper. But then, just when you had relaxed, thinking: "Go on, Chippy, stick that in," he would knock the ball square to you. More often than not, the ball would hit your foot, and go wide.

On another occasion, with him 25 yards out from goal, and me in space screaming for a pass, he would look up, shape as if to knock a through ball, then blast a shot into the top corner of the net.

He was so good — the most talented team-mate I have ever had — that you'd have to smile. Otherwise, you'd be climbing the walls!

BOBBY MOORE, whom I played with for England towards the end of his international career, was another exceptional passer.

95

He would see runs very quickly and could play the ball straight to your feet with perfect timing. He gave me vast freedom as a player. His quality of passing encouraged me to make runs which I would not have made, perhaps, had a lesser player been in possession.

That is why you should never worry when asked to play at a higher level with unfamiliar team-mates. While you won't have an intimate knowledge of their strengths and weaknesses, their greater ability should take much of the pressure from you.

I always found it easier to score goals in the First Division than the Second, simply because I was playing in better teams.

Alan Hudson's passing.

ALAN HUDSON was another man I first met on the international field, although we later became club-mates at Arsenal.

He had one astounding skill. Alan would run at a defender, drawing him in, and it would look to all the world as if he were about to pass in a certain way. Then suddenly, he would flick the ball on his blind side to a player — often me — running into his path.

His timing had to be perfect and usually was. Often you would be making the "blind" run and thinking: "Alan, you have left it too late!" when the ball would appear at your feet, with the defence caught out of position.

He could also pass a ball while looking and shaping the other way, just by changing the angle of his foot. Brilliant.

MIKE KEEN, one of my Luton colleagues, had long, gangly legs and played at right-half. Naturally, he was very right footed and would often get in an inside-right shooting position.

He had a fair shot, but I noticed that he would often pull his effort wide of the far post. Therefore, as soon as he got in a shooting position, I would run towards the left wing corner flag, then check my run to head diagonally towards the far post, so that I would arrive in time for a tap-in.

Over two seasons, I scored two goals that way. It might not seem much, but if you grab a goal a season from every other outfield player, that's nine for a start!

Mike Keen's shooting.

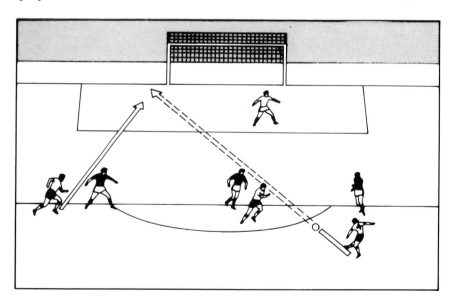

Opponents

MARTIN BUCHAN, of Manchester United and Scotland, was very quick and would always drop off and give you space to run at him. Even if you pushed back onto him, then came off to receive the pass, he was quite happy to let you go.

ALAN KENNEDY, a former team-mate at Newcastle — and an opponent at Liverpool — is a super player. But, like everyone else, he does have at least one flaw which can be exploited.

Alan Kennedy's positioning.

During his career with Newcastle, Alan tended to move too far forward, towards the ball, for crosses to the far post, which meant that the ball would often go over him. He would do this so often that, when playing against him for Arsenal, I would never even have to watch for the cross. I would time my run and jump from Alan's movements.

I would move forward, and when he came with me, I'd suddenly check to connect with the ball a yard behind him.

This aspect of Alan's game has been rather less noticeable at Liverpool, mainly I think because of the way the team play. Defensively a lot of teams try to deny opponents the scope to get into dangerous crossing positions, but Liverpool are masters of the art.

PHIL THOMPSON, who captained Liverpool during my playing days, hated garlic! That's why I used to eat loads of it the night before I was due to play against him. The first time he came near me, I would breathe all over him. "Get off, Mal," he would cry, "What the hell have you been eating!"

He then gave me three yards of space throughout the game!

WILLIE McFAUL, a former opposing goalkeeper, who became a club-mate when I joined Newcastle, also had a strange quirk. He hated people treading on his feet!

So, whenever we won a corner I made a bee-line for Willie and would tread gently on his toes. Not a great big step, just a tender tap, tap, tap. "Oh, get off!" he'd shout and lose all concentration!

PETER SHILTON, England's No. 1 goalkeeper was like Dracula when I played against him — he hated crosses!

I discovered that if you put him under pressure from crosses, his general standard — normally the highest in Britain — would drop. Finally, he would get caught in no-man's land on a high ball, allowing me to sneak in and grab a goal.

99

ALAN STEVENSON, Burnley's goalkeeper, had a habit of leaning slightly backwards, putting his weight on his heels. Therefore, he couldn't move forward from the waist and any shot near his body was almost impossible to reach.

In under four weeks towards the end of season 1973-74, Newcastle played Burnley four times — two League matches, the Texaco Cup Final and an FA Cup semi-final — and I scored in each match, including two in the semi-final.

Every goal was the same. I was put clear and, as Stevenson advanced, hit my shot within two feet of his legs.

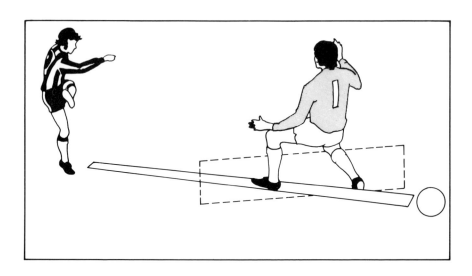

My shooting target against Alan Stevenson.

The main thing is not to worry about opponents' strengths, but work on their weaknesses. The more limited your own skills, the more you need to concentrate on the failings of others.

Pace will panic some centre-halves while others will view it with a shrug of the shoulders.

Many have a favourite tackling foot, normally their right, so if you work hard on your right foot, you will be able to attack them on their left.

How well you exploit those weaknesses is dependant on how hard you are prepared to work. I warn you, it's not easy.

If I was poor at a particular skill, I wouldn't attempt it. Not in a proper match, anyway. But don't restrict yourself too much. All the while you test the centre-half, you are also testing yourself, finding new ways, new barriers. Never be happy to be what you are — never get complacent.

Learn to think for yourself. Today, unfortunately, is the era of the coach. The all-seeing powers, the men who believe they do all the thinking for their players.

I find it distressing that so many players are willing to accept this reasoning. They tend to leave all football theory to their coach, and never think things through on their own. Therefore, there is a blank acceptance of the coaches' doctrines, many of which are negative.

As I've said, coaches like balls to be played the way you are facing, to keep possession. They don't like players who turn and run at goal. But if you feel you are capable of this form of exciting play — do it! Don't listen to the coaches — don't take the easy way out.

Goalscorers are becoming few and far between, because fewer players are giving thought to their trade — and all goalscorers have to do that.

They have to be the last players off the training field. They've got to be greedy and demand the utmost help and co-operation from team-mates.

When operating in pairs, the greedier of the two strikers always goes to the post that the ball should go to. The other goes on a decoy run — Frank Stapleton, only a young lad when we played together at Arsenal, made a hell of a lot of decoy runs! He was probably a much better far post header than I, but if the ball looked like arriving there, he would always be sent on a near post run.

If you keep playing on percentages that a chance will come off, sooner or later one will.

Even when you've absorbed all the advice in this chapter, don't expect everything to go right.

I recall that before playing for England against Wales, Rodney Marsh — who I had admired from the Fulham terraces as a teenager — said to me: "Look, Mal, you're quick, they're slow at the back. If you run wide, how do you cross the ball?"

"I always drive it hard and low," I replied.

Midway through the second-half, I got the ball to the dead-ball line and was about to cross. Rodney was sprinting in unmarked at the near post, ready for the "hard and low" cross — but I slipped, my foot went under the ball and I knocked a perfect chip to the far post.

Rodney was left looking a complete idiot in front of the Ninion Park crowd.

He looked across in despair. "Cheers, Mal," he mumbled!

8 · Playing to Strengths

Having stressed the importance of making great demands upon your team-mates, I should add that a goalscorer must be even more critical of himself.

It is an extremely unpleasant experience to pick faults in your own game — but every great player has, at one time, put himself through the most stringent self-analysis.

There are thousands of different facets to football — at least 100 to each position — and it is virtually impossible for a player to be good at everything. You will be good at some things, average at others and weak at still more. A goalscorer has to make a list and decide where his strengths lie.

You might finish with perhaps four or five strongpoints, two average attributes and a list of weaknesses as long as the Forth Bridge. That doesn't matter, providing you put your strengths to the correct use.

It's no use kidding yourself that you are good at something if you are not while, at the same time, it is pointless being unnecessarily modest in your assessments.

Having done this, many players make the mistake of trying to improve their weaknesses to the detriment of their strengths, finishing up ordinary at everything.

The best way is to work tirelessly at your strengths, making them so absolute, so strong that, when put into use, they are virtually unstoppable.

It is far better to be a master of one craft than a "jack-of-all-trades". If you have a good left-foot, as I had, work until it is the best in the land. Then you can worry about achieving power with your right.

If you're 6 foot 3 inches and not very quick, it is pointless trying to improve your speed over short distances, and forgetting to develop your jumping power.

You should be practicing night and day, getting your arms up, jumping, springing from the knees, jacking forward from the hips until there is not a centre-half in the land with a hope of beating you to a cross.

Then — and only then — can you begin to improve your pace. Become great at what you're good at, so your strengths more than cover for your weaknesses.

Remember, your team-mates will play passes to suit you and, if they don't, tell them they're wrong.

This applies to all positions. You should be watching for opponents not playing to *their* strengths and, if that's the case, then exploit them unmercifully. For example, if a slow marker has come tight, try to turn or spin him.

But first, work on yourself. Take out a pen and paper and see what your own list comprises. The best way for me to show you how this is done, is by analysing myself — after all, that is what I spent a career doing!

MALCOLM MACDONALD

Strengths
Speed
Strength on ball
Powerful left foot
Strong in the air, although not very tall
Single-mindedness to score goals

Weaknesses
Control
Stamina
Height (not tall enough to pose a consistent
   aerial threat).
Not a good tactical player with regard to
   working for a team — my single-
   mindedness to score goals meant I was too
   selfish

So my basic strengths were speed, coupled
with a good shot. Having realised this, I had
to form a shield to hide my faults. In other
words, my strengths had to be good enough
to make me a force against any opponents.

To achieve this, I relied a great deal on my
team-mates, as well as my own assessment of
what I could and couldn't do.

As time went on, my list changed. By the
time I was in my late 20s my control improved vastly — but I wasn't as quick as I had
been. Thus, I altered my objectives accordingly and made different demands on my
team-mates.

Everything I did was intended to benefit
me in my quest to score goals. Now, I will
analyse four famous players — as I once
analysed myself — in search of an answer to
this simple question: why haven't they
scored more goals?

Each has differing strengths and weaknesses, and I will make allowance for any changes that occurred during their playing careers. The four are: Frank Stapleton, Andy Gray, Kevin Keegan and Johann Cruyff.

FRANK STAPLETON
(Arsenal, Manchester United and Eire)

Strengths
Aerial power
Strength on ball
Courage
Tireless and determined worker
Makes excellent wide runs

Weaknesses
Slow
Control
Scruffy kicker of the ball
Sometimes goes too wide for too long

I partnered Frank in the Arsenal forward line during his first three years in professional football and can claim to know him as well as anyone as a player.

When he joined the Gunners as a raw youngster from Dublin, he was a poor kicker of the ball and his touch frequently let him down. But he was exceptional in the air and, had a marvellous attitude to the game in terms of his willingness to work.

Frank took a long, hard look in the mirror and thought: "This is what I'm good at, I'll become better. This is what I'm bad at, I'll improve."

The only thing he could do nothing about was his pace, Frank has always been rather slow, and it could be that he decided: "I'm not quick enough to get there as many times as I would like but, by everything I do, I'll make my partner the finest goalscorer in the land."

Frank Stapleton. A great striker, but not goalscorer.
(Allsport)

That perhaps, might go some way towards explaining why Frank, is *not* an out-and-out goalscorer.

He concentrated on his weaknesses more than his strengths and has become an outstanding all-round forward. He is still excellent in the air and a talented positional runner who will work endlessly to create space and give team-mates scoring chances. He still holds people off well, has very good close control and a few tricks up his sleeve.

In fact, if I had to recommend one striker for youngsters to watch it would be Frank.

He is the ideal man to partner a goalscorer and, indeed, we dovetailed superbly at Arsenal, where I was the "comedian" and him the feed. I would be very cruel in the way I made him work for me — I can even remember calling him my "dog" once! — but he was a willing and intelligent listener, with dedication and ambition.

My attitude was that I would score the goals, while Frank would learn the trade. Having done that, he put all his talents and strengths to work, and got the best out of himself.

He also scored a fair amount of goals — but he's no *goalscorer*.

ANDY GRAY
(Dundee United, Aston Villa, Wolves, Everton and Scotland)

Strengths
Good in the air
Good positional sense
Brave
Good attitude — very keen, very hard-working

Weaknesses
Slow
Control
Ungainly

Andy Gray had one phenomenal season, playing for Aston Villa in 1976-77. At the end of it, he was voted both Player of the Year and Young Player of the Year by the Professional Footballers' Association. It is a unique double, because the following year the rules were changed so that it was impossible for one man to take both awards.

Andy scored 26 goals in 37 League games — and 29 overall that season.

During the summer of 1977, a friend re-

Andy Gray. Too much effort.
(Allsport)

marked to me that Gray's achievement proved that he was a great striker.

"Yes," I replied, "he has done extremely well. But I don't think he'll do it again."

The reason was that Gray, in striving to prove himself in the Football League, had repeatedly thrown himself in where the proverbial angels feared to tread and, at times, been so reckless and fearless that it sent a chill up the spine. I couldn't see one man having the willpower to do that again. Of course, you need effort and determination to be a goalscorer — but the actual scoring aspect should be effortless. In Gray's case, there was effort etched into every inch of his body and, for me, that had to take its toll.

I think I have been proved right, even though Gray had a marvellous 1974/5 season for Everton, and played a big part in them winning the Championship and European Cup-Winners Cup.

I've never seen in Gray what I've seen in great goalscorers like Bryan "Pop" Robson.

Robson, a quiet, unobtrusive character off the field, pounced on chances with the stealth of a born hunter. Andy Gray, however, is a trier, not a hunter. He lost that special appetite for goals after that great season at Villa and had to wait a long time for it to return, with Everton. But the mark of a true goalscorer is that the sparkle *never* dims.

KEVIN KEEGAN
(Scunthorpe, Liverpool, SV Hamburg, Southampton, Newcastle and England)

Strengths
Quick, without being electric
Good control
Exceptionally strong in the air, for a little man
Quick-thinking brain
Innovative skills and flicks
Hard working
Tremendous stamina
Played within limitations

Weaknesses
Not an accurate shot
Desired to be a great footballer, not a
    goalscorer

I would rate Kevin as one of the most improved players the Football League has

Kevin Keegan. An out-standing example of the self-made player.
(Hailey Sports)

ever known. Certainly, the Kevin Keegan who signed for Liverpool in May 1971 bore no resemblance to the man who retired from football at Newcastle, 13 years later.

Initially, he wasn't particularly quick, his control wasn't exceptional, his shot wasn't good and he wasn't strong in the air.

But he worked hard, harder than any professional I have ever known, and became good at all of these things — and more!

In fact, by the end of his career, his mind was so alive with ideas and invention that he left team-mates at Second Division Newcastle standing.

He utilised the most superb little flicks and created goals when they seemed least likely.

But he only scored 171 goals — a total unrepresentative of his ability. The reason was that his dedication to becoming a great footballer was such, that scoring goals went by the wayside. By the time he had satisfied his original desire, to become a great footballer, his body was too exhausted to become an out-and-out goalscorer.

JOHANN CRUYFF
(Ajax, Feyenoord, Barcelona and Holland)

Strengths
Shooting
Speed
Control
Dribbling
Taking people on
His left foot
His right foot
Heading
Courage
Passing
Curling the ball
Strength on the ball
Stamina

Weaknesses
?

That list says it all. Johann Cruyff was *too* good to be a goalscorer. He was such a brilliant footballer, with enough energy and stamina to go all over the place, that to restrict himself to merely scoring would have been crazy!

9 · Positioning

Positioning in relation to your forward partner or partners is governed in the main by the pattern of play adopted by your team.

There are three basic formations: 4-3-3, 4-4-2 and 4-2-4. All require different objectives, methods and positioning.

4-3-3 is normally played with a winger on one flank, and two forwards playing in more central areas. Unfortunately, this tactic is dying out and, if you do use a wide man, many coaches prefer to play him from deep — a variation of 4-4-2.

Indeed, 4-4-2 can, theoretically, include two wingers when in attack, reverting to midfield when possession has been lost.

Other than that, the most conventional system is to have two target-men, supported by midfielders.

Both 4-3-3 without a winger (using three interchanging forwards) and 4-2-4 (two central strikers, two wingers) were formations I hated, as I found that the middle of the pitch became very crowded and it was difficult for me to create and find space.

It is always important that goalscorers have the room to manoeuvre and create opportunities.

Defenders invariably become panicky when isolated from colleagues, because the forward has more options open to him. Few defenders relish one-to-one confrontations. They like to have the "insurance" of players covering them.

4-3-3

If this is played with a winger who is getting enough of the ball and doing his job properly, you'll be on the receiving end of many crosses, and therefore one of the two centre-forwards should be a big, strong-in-the-air type like Frank Stapleton or Peter Withe.

His partner is most commonly a smaller man, making runs off the big fellow and waiting for the flick downs and knock-ons in the box.

During the general build-up play, the big man will be the furthest forward, with the little man slightly behind, so he can run onto the flick or a pass beyond the defence, from an onside position.

A variation on this is for a defender to hit a long ball up to the big man who, having controlled it, plays it into the path of an advancing midfielder. The latter then plays a through ball for the second forward to run onto. The timing must be split-second perfect, especially on the part of the second forward. He has to be in a position in which he can avoid being caught offside at the time the final pass is made, and to make it possible for him to beat any retreating defenders to the ball.

Around the edge of the area, the midfielders should provide sufficient support to enable them to get to knock-downs, but if any

*4-3-3, with a winger.
With the winger being
supported by the mid-
field player and full-
back, the two strikers
start their move to get
on the end of a cross by
running away!*
*Remember what I said
earlier about the import-
ance of making angled
or curved runs?*

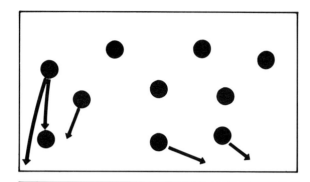

*4-3-3, without a winger.
Two quick, mobile
strikers making runs of
a big, target-man centre
forward, with the two
wide midfielders
providing the attacking
width.*

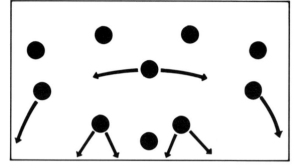

*4-4-2. A system I always
liked, simply because the
strikers have so much
space to work in.*

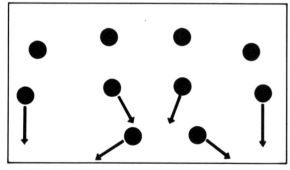

*4-2-4- A system I hated,
for the opposite reason!*

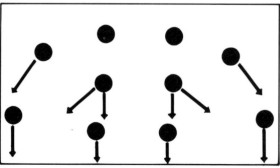

116

of them attempt to actually run onto the through-ball, they will almost certainly be foiled by the goalkeeper coming off his line.

As for the smaller of the two forwards, it is a waste of time being in the vicinity of his forward partner, and thus he should take up a wider position and look for the angled approach to goal.

This angle at goal should always be from the opposite flank to the ball. Invariably, possession will go to the winger, so the forward has an ideal run on goal for the cross.

Usually, when playing the ball to the wings, the big man is in the middle, the little man outside the far post. These two must switch, the larger forward taking up a position ready to "attack" the far post, his smaller partner making a near post run.

How to pull defenders around when going for balls to the near and far post. In this instance, for example, defenders would be expecting striker A to go to the near post and B to the far post.

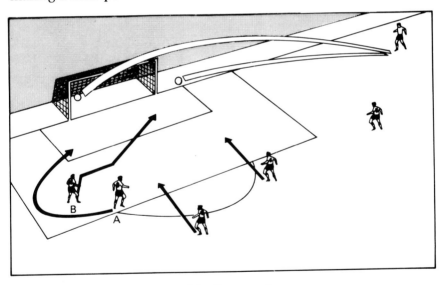

The near post run should distract the defence — taking pressure from the aerial target man — and, when the ball goes to the far post, the little man should run out, then in again — in a "V"-shape — to pounce on any knock-down.

117

Near post crosses are seldom used. Certainly, they are not as effective as they were in the mid-'70s, when West Ham's Martin Peters repeatedly scored from them. He had the uncanny ability to glide into the area, unnoticed by the defence — hence his nickname 'The Ghost'. Since then, defences have got wise to this ploy, and will cover the near post with a tall defender, or midfielder.

If you get a chance of a near post header, meet the cross in line with the post, giving the ball a powerful flick — somewhere between a glance and a full-bodied header.

By working with your partner, you should get to know what form his knock-downs will take, but you must also be prepared to change direction at an instant for the ball coming off the woodwork or a defender.

The best way to practice this sudden change in direction is to draw two lines, three yards apart, and run in between, touching one, then the other with your nearest foot. Remember to practice your turns both ways (right to left, left to right). All this will also teach you to check quickly so as to lose your marker.

A 4-3-3 system with three forwards means having two target-men and a runner — or two runners and a target-man — and the runner(s) will usually operate a little deeper in search of the knockdowns. But, as I have said, it makes the centre of the field very crowded.

Genuine width is difficult to create, and often you will find two, sometimes three, forwards in the same area of the pitch, trying to do the same job!

4-4-2

This system creates tremendous options for a forward. He'll be playing ahead of two central midfielders and two wide midfielders. But the flankmen, though ready to move into forward positions, are not filling any of the forwards' space across the width of the pitch.

Your positional play is partly governed by the defensive tactics used by the opposition. For example, they might push both the full-backs forward to mark the wide midfielders. Therefore, the space to exploit is the area vacated by the full-backs.

If both forwards occupy central positions close to each other, they minimise the target for players hitting a pass. Also, one midfield player, through good positioning in front of the two strikers, can block the pass to either.

In the middle of the field, the centre-half usually marks on a diagonal outside position. When standing wide he will get on an angle between you and the goal. This will leave space wide, so the full-backs may be pulled down the field to take up space in the holes, leaving you half-marked by both centre and full back.

Two forwards operating through the middle will have to interchange or make the occasional spurt into wide positions. In other words, only by changing their own positions will they discover where the defenders will and won't go, and where space can be found.

Also, it's important to bear in mind that goals are rarely scored through the middle of the park. That's why I would say that 90 out of 100 forwards prefer to play wide when using 4-4-2.

When the ball is put into the net in front of goal, you will invariably find that it has come in from a wide position. Therefore, the forwards playing the wide game cease to have a partnership outside the area, but form a triangle with the two midfielders on the latter's side of the pitch.

Liverpool are perhaps the best example of a team who use these triangles correctly — they employ a striker with the outside right and the inside right, for instance, and on the other flank, the other striker with the outside and inside left.

To combat this, the opposing coach will often use three centre-halves, two marking the forward points of the two triangles, with the third acting as a spare man or "sweeper" behind. The full-backs, in this instance, would move forward to become wide-midfield players.

Liverpool's 4-4-2 system. When you look at the angles they create, it's hardly surprising that they often appear to outnumber opponents in all parts of the field, and that each player rarely needs more than one or two touches on the ball. It's like watching a team practising their first-time passing in training, with a circle of nine players and two in the middle leading the session.

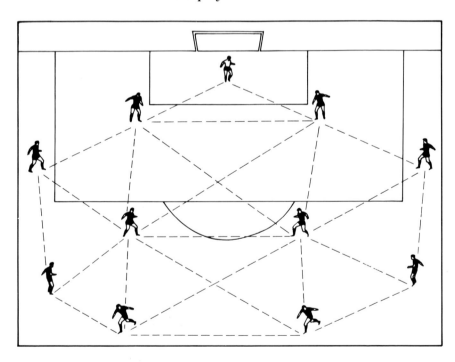

It is important in this instance that you and your fellow striker play a great distance apart, thus making it impossible for the sweeper to cover both his centre halves. One of you will be in a "one-against-one" situation, so that ability to "spin" around your marker is all-important.

You can also run your marker wide, then bend inside him towards goal. Variety is needed to unsettle the defender, so take him wide, central, and to the other wing, just to see where he is prepared to go.

The covering centre-half will be a little deeper, but still needs to be tested. Check back behind him, check inside, check outside, run one way then switch to the other — always make your game unpredictable.

By turning abruptly inside the marking centre half, you will cut across his line in a run directly at the covering defender. With 4-4-2 there is a lot of room for the goalscorer to experiment with little runs and checks — test your man out all the time.

You can even switch flanks with your partner to see if the markers will follow — if they don't, they are probably playing a zonal system. Discover what foot your marker favours, then attack him on his other side.

It is probably the most enjoyable way for a forward to operate, but depends on good support from midfield. Don't allow colleagues to run into your space, but their back up once the ball has been played forward must be instant.

Once this has been done, you can even run across the field, letting your space be filled by the midfielder. This will cause your marker to either leave you or the midfielder unmarked, or be caught in a no-man's land between the two of you.

Why I loved being a front man in a 4-4-2 system. Look at the scope you get to lose your marker, without bumping into one of your team-mates! In the situation shown here I particularly favoured the second type of run. It gave me a better chance of keeping onside, and of leaving my marker stranded in no man's land.

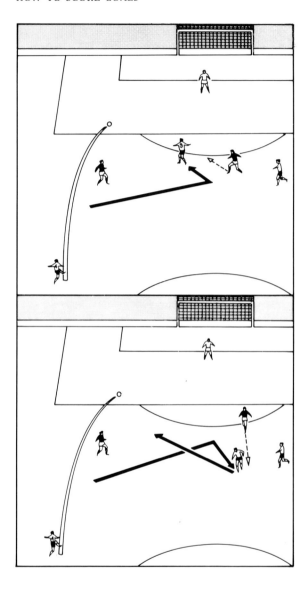

4-2-4 or The Long Ball Game

My own difficulties in adapting to this system have unfortunately prejudiced me against it — and I still maintain it is often the kiss of death for a potential goalscorer.

Two forwards operate with two wingers, and the flankmen must be told to tightly hug the sideline, because once they move inside, so do their markers. Eight bodies in the middle of the park can have a disastrous effect on your ability to find space.

When using a 4-2-4 system, teams often start using a long-ball game, and it becomes very difficult for them to play balls to the front-men's feet, unless the wingers drop back. Watford are perhaps the best example, using two nippy wide men, with a big centre-forward and a little man looking for the knockdowns.

I only ever found joy with this system by stretching the defence across the full width of the pitch — which 4-2-4 does naturally — and exploiting the space behind the full-backs.

But, whether intentionally or otherwise, all teams have to play the long-ball tactic *some-time* during the game.

It stretches the play, forcing the defence to drop off, so you have more room to push forward without being caught offside. You can exploit channels created between the forward line and the centre-half, and beyond the defence, while also giving wingers the chance to take people on.

But the opposing penalty area does get very cramped, and you have to be very alert to capitalise on the bagatelle situations that develop there, with the ball whizzing about as if it were on a pinball machine. You have to be "alive" when the ball comes, and you have to be prepared to shoot through bodies.

You'll have days when you never get a sniff of a chance, and others when you get many opportunities. This is probably the best situation in which to sharpen your "radar" ... but don't just stand there! Run in and shoot in one action. Practice shooting in your stride — quick little steps, then BANG!

To be quick in the area, you must take short strides. Watch sprinters — over the first ten yards, when they are gaining acceleration, they'll probably take 20 steps. Your action must be the same, as quick as you can get it, because sprinting is vital for a goalscorer.

Positioning around the area. The dotted line is the angle of the attack, the broken line the striker's angle of vision. You may remember that I have already touched on this point, on page 74. I can't stress it enough.

Positioning in and around the area

One golden rule when attacking the penalty area, to connect with a cross or pass, is to create an angle of vision for yourself that incorporates your two targets — the goal and the ball. As you can see in the diagram, the striker has pulled away from the ball,

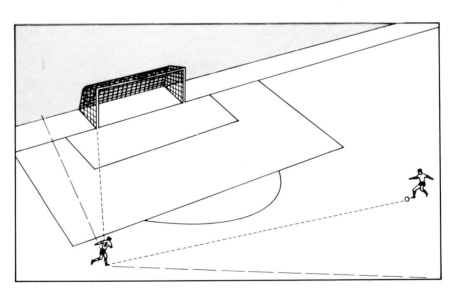

towards the left flank, and in so doing, has opened his number of options to the maximum.

When you are coming in at the far post, make sure your run is angled and late, bearing in mind that you can make up ground going forward but never backwards.

One further thing to remember is the "banshee effect". When you're going for a ball, scream like mad to put defenders off.

Never call "My ball!" because you'll give away a free-kick for "ungentlemanly conduct"; instead, shout "centre-forward's ball!" or your own name. This will show if the defender is brave and, if he is not, is liable to destroy his confidence completely!

Your marker might be 6.5 but I'll wager he jumps 5.6 if he thinks some whirling dervish is going to clatter him.

The main thing with all positioning in and around the area is: never give up on a ball! Always keep going because you'll be amazed how many times a supposed "lost cause" can be retrieved.

10 · Set Pieces

So far, I have given advice on how to score goals in open play. Now for the art of putting the ball in the net from set pieces — free kicks, corners and even throw-ins.

All you need is a bit of imagination, ingenuity ... and the willingness to practice.

The pros spend a lot of time in training on perfecting free-kick moves, and here are some for your team to try ....

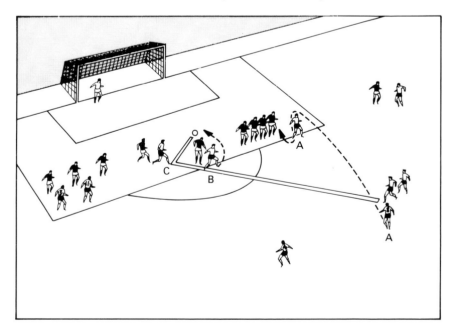

1.   Fulham had a lot of success with this one when I was manager there. Forward A dummies over the ball and makes a run wide of the defensive "wall". Suddenly, he stops and walks back towards the ball, gesticulating at his team-mates around the ball as if they have caused the move to go wrong. The wider of the two players on the ball, B, then plays it as shown and forward A spins and runs behind the wall for the lay-off (making sure that his timing keeps him on-side at the time of the final pass).

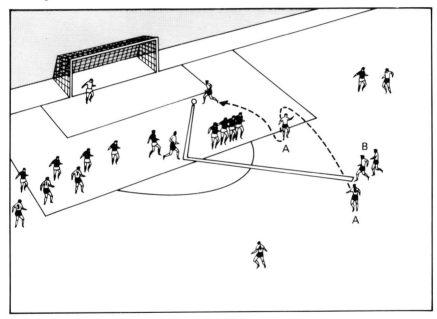

2.   Another memorable free kick — a variation on the previous one — from my spell as Fulham manager. Player A dummies over the ball, and gives the impression that he is going to run around the wall — only to stop and turn back. As before, the ball is hit to the central striker, B, but instead of laying it off behind the wall, he dummies over it and spins, thus allowing the forward behind, C, to gently strike it into his path.

3.   The man on the ball, A, shapes to cross the ball, but stops. This provides an "excuse" for a feigned argument with the forwards who, having made their runs and taken their markers with them, make a big show of remonstrating with him. While all this is going on, though, the left back, B, quickly sneaks around the back of everyone. The cross is then hit over all the forwards and defenders, and beyond the goalkeeper's reach, the full back heads it across the face of the goal ... and there is the alert striker, C, with a great chance to apply the finishing touch.

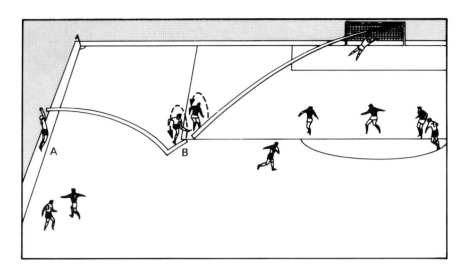

4. This is the sort of near-post corner which, you might recall, has been used so successfully by the England team in recent years. The ball is played to the near post, where one of your tallest players A (in England's case, it has usually been Terry Butcher) will flick it on for B. Note that the scorer has suddenly come off the line, thus ensuring that he can "attack" the flick-on properly.

5.   Throw-ins aren't taken seriously enough in my view. Generally, they are looked upon as just a means of getting an attack started — but, in fact, they can produce a fair number of goals.

For example, I remember a goal I scored for Newcastle in an F.A. Cup tie against Bolton. My left foot was generally regarded as being far more effective than my right, and therefore defenders would be quite happy for me to get the ball on the latter side. For one of our throw-ins against Bolton, I dummied to go down the left touchline, but checked back and hit a right foot volley into the net.

Players with a long throw — who can propel the ball into the goalmouth from 15-20 yards — can cause particular problems. Many Chelsea fans must still remember the throw from Ian Hutchinson which led to David Webb scoring the winning goal against Leeds in the 1970 F.A. Cup Final.

11 · My Ten Greatest Goal-scorers

This is probably the hardest chapter to write in the entire book. Over a century of goals and goalscorers, and I have foolishly restricted myself to a mere ten.

So who to put in? Who to leave out?

Many, such as Steve Bloomer and Jimmy McGrory, are just names to me. Legends still mentioned with reverence in Derby and Glasgow.

Others, such as Alfredo di Stefano, were men glimpsed on television, the knowledge of their infinite prowess having been passed by word of mouth and newspaper reports.

I have therefore kept my selection to the past 25 years — when I have studied football and goalscorers — and make no apologies for any British bias.

After all, I am more familiar with the records and performances of men from the U.K., than those from, say, South America or the Continent.

Finally, the list runs in no particular order, all are respected as strikers who have given inestimable pleasure to myself, and thousands of other football fans.

The incomparable Jimmy Greaves.
(Allsport)

JIMMY GREAVES
(Chelsea, AC Milan, Tottenham, West Ham and England)

133

So far, I have refrained from talking of "natural" goalscorers — if all goalscorers were "naturals", books such as this would be unnecessary! But, if such a thing exists, it was personified by Jimmy Greaves.

I don't think he could put into words just how he scored his goals, yet by the time he retired he had netted 357 times in 517 League matches, adding another 44 in 57 international games.

He was felled by an attack of hepatitis — a strain of jaundice — in 1965, after which he reckoned he was never as fast again. Therefore, it is possible that Greaves could have increased his goal total considerably.

To see him in his earliest days at Chelsea, one would have thought he was most in need of a hot dinner! With his wiry, 5ft 8in frame, (accentuated by his baggy, knee-length shorts), he looked a little boy lost — until he got the ball at his feet!

Then, he would explode into action, opening up defences with a startling run, dummying defenders and goalkeepers alike with a dip of the shoulder.

He was the most economic mover I have ever seen. Frighteningly fast, yet his short legs and short steps gave the impression that he was never exerting himself.

He had such wonderful timing. He would stand still in the area, then suddenly dart for the ball and just as quickly despatch it into the back of the net.

His shots never seemed to have great power, yet they always got there, with an unerring accuracy for nestling just inside a post.

He had a hunger for goals, a great need that never seemed to be satisfied with merely one or two.

Ted Drake, his manager at Chelsea, said of him: "I knew Jimmy was something special when he scored 114 goals in his last season as a Youth team player. I remember congratulating him for scoring seven in one match — the next week he went out and scored eight!"

That was a scene well-known at Stamford Bridge. Greaves scored five goals against Wolves, Preston and West Bromwich Albion; four against Portsmouth, Newcastle and Nottingham Forest, *and* helped himself to another nine hat-tricks. And all in four, fabulous, years.

Like many of the greatest goalscorers, he was never one for training or coaches. In 1968, he asked England manager Alf Ramsey to be left out of the side. "I simply told him I was not to be considered for his training get-togethers if he was not going to play me in the side," Jimmy said. "I never had much time for tactical talks."

It is unlikely we will see his kind again. His name, I am sure, will stand forever as the greatest English goalscorer.

GERD MULLER
(West Germany)

If Gerd Muller had retired in 1971 — at the age of 26 — he would still have gone into the record books as the finest European goalscorer of the post-war era.

Up to then, he had scored 33 goals in 29 internationals, and 152 in six League seasons for Bayern Munich. In the 1970 World Cup he was top scorer with ten goals, and in the 1969-70 season he won Europe's Golden Boots award with 38 goals.

In fact, the word "striker" could have been invented for him.

Yet, when I first saw Muller in the white shirt of West Germany, I could hardly believe he had the guts to walk on a football field at all!

135

He couldn't run properly, he was slow, awkward, a bad kicker of the ball and, when I expected him to come alive with the ball at his feet, he didn't!

But he got past people, poked, prodded, scored a sackful of goals and made the penalty area his domain in a way unsurpassed by any goalscorer before or since.

Perhaps the classic Muller goal was the one which knocked England out of the 1970 World Cup at the quarter-final stage.

Lohr headed back across England's goal, Brian Labone could not get his head to the ball and Muller, sensing this, moved into free space, twisting his thick-set body to hook the dropping ball past goalkeeper Peter Bonetti.

While many would have challenged Labone to an aerial duel, Muller knew exactly where the ball would be, *and* the best way to attack it.

Looking scruffy and unfit he would lull defenders into a false sense of security — and then pounce!

Apparently, when Muller first moved to Bayern Munich in 1963, the club coach, Yugoslav international 'Tshik' Cajkovski told Wilhelm Neudecker, the club president: "I am not putting this bear among my racehorses!"

This is typical of the lack of understanding exhibited by coaches towards goalscorers.

Muller was more of a racehorse than any of them. He might have looked like an old nag, but his reflexes and co-ordination were second to none.

He had rare powers of anticipation allowing him to assess a situation immediately and shoot on goal, without giving the defence any indication of his intention.

At 5 ft 8 in — like Greaves — he was small enough to trouble defenders — and strong enough to avoid being pushed off the ball. He had the ideal build for a goalscorer.

I've never seen him hit a shot that hasn't bounced before hitting the net, and rarely have I seen him score from outside the box.

One of these occasions was the match at Wembley in 1972. I watched in the stand amazed. Muller didn't touch the ball until it was within five yards of the penalty area — it was as if his team-mates had said to him: "Don't get involved in the game. Hang around the box, we'll get the ball to you, and you stick it in the net." He was a man alone — yet the Germans loved him for it.

As for that goal from outside the area against England, the ball bounced at least twice before it crossed the line, and even then, barely disturbed the net. But he had done his job — West Germany won 3-1.

When he scored, I would often think: "You lucky so and so." But he did it too many times to be lucky. He would flit in and out of space, nip in front of people and, with the tiniest deflection, knock the ball gently into the corner of the net.

As with Greaves, I cannot remember him missing; he turned goalscoring into an art form.

To some, he may have been a bear among racehorses, but I am sure even Simon Smith's bear wasn't *this* talented!

Muller, too, could not explain his extraordinary ability.

"Somehow, something inside tells me 'Gerd go this way, Gerd go that way' and the ball comes over and I score," he said. "That's not a very satisfactory explanation, I know, but I can't do any better.

"Maybe it's just as well. After all, if I don't know how to do it, no-one can discover how to stop me!"

Bryan "Pop" Robson –
a superb volleyer.
(Hailey Sports)

BRYAN "POP" ROBSON
(Newcastle, West Ham, Sunderland, Carlisle, Chelsea)

When "Pop" Robson left Newcastle in season 1970-71, I was brought in as his replacement — one hell of a hard act to follow! A short while later, when he was in the north-east, we did a training session together.

The goalkeeper was Martin Burley, and we got two of the younger apprentices to stand on each wing knocking balls in. We stood in the middle and took turns to strike at goal.

We covered everything — volleys, straight drives, with the inside of the foot and the outside of the foot, chips, flicks — the lot!

We were enjoying ourselves so much that we could easily have stayed out there all day. It was Martin Burley who called a halt to that session. "Look," he said, "you might be having fun, but you've hit over 1,000 shots at me. Those poor apprentices can hardly lift a leg and I'm totally exhausted. I'm going in!"

I remember that experience as one probably similar to playing John McEnroe at tennis. You know you're not going to beat him — but you'll learn a lot by trying!

Actually, Pop and I did keep a count of our goals. He beat me by 12.

He was without doubt the best goalscorer I have seen from the edge of the box. A beautifully sweet striker of the ball, with a short backswing.

During that training session, I noticed that "Pop" could repeatedly strike a volley to exactly the same spot.

In a match I played for Newcastle against West Ham, the ball came to him outside the area, a foot off the ground, just inside the near post. He readjusted his stance and, with as little movement as possible, smashed the ball into the roof of the net.

It was such a good goal that even I found myself applauding.

He scored goals at every level, against every defence and goalkeeper going, and still, at the age of 38, kept playing and never lost his hunger for scoring.

"Seeing and hearing the ball hit the back of the net is like a drug to me," he said. "I'm totally hooked on the thrill it brings."

Yet — like Greaves, Muller and many of my top ten — you wouldn't notice him if he passed you in the street. Thick-set and balding, he was under no illusions about his physical ability.

"Over a hundred-yard sprint, most blokes could leave me standing," he said. "But I've got speed where it counts — over three, four yards — to give me the vital edge on defenders."

That Pop was still scoring goals at the age of 38 — in fact, he got his 300th in the 1983/84 season — is proof enough that appearances count for nothing in this game.

PELE (Brazil)

Pele is probably the most well-known footballer to ever draw breath. Known simply as "The King", he had the most incredible range of skills and scored over 1,000 goals in his brilliant career.

In the words of Jaoa Saldanha, the former Brazilian team manager: "If you ask me who is the best full-back in Brazil, I will say Pele. If you ask who is the best wing-half, I would say Pele. Who is the best winger? Pele. If you ask me who is the best goalkeeper, I would probably have to say Pele. He is like no other footballer. He is to our team what Shakespeare is to English literature."

Scottish wing-half Pat Crerand maintained that the word Pele should be spelt "G-O-D"

Pele – a one-man team.
(Allsport)

and even Bobby Moore, no under-achiever when it came to cutting out the best goalscorers in the game, paid homage to his unique talents.

"Sometimes I tackled him and I was convinced I had won the ball," he said. "I felt solid contact with it, and was sure it was mine. Then I looked round and he was ten yards away with the ball at his feet. He had played it against my legs, and picked up the rebound as if nothing had happened.

"The first time I thought it had been an accident. But, after six or seven such 'accidents' I realised he was doing it on purpose. Nothing was too outrageous for him."

It is hard to find words that can express just how good this man was, to those who did not see him play. He had the lot, and did the lot — every skill in the book, plus a few never before attempted.

I once saw a film of his career and, if you ever get the chance to watch this hour-long documentary, I would advise you to do the same. It takes you from his childhood through to his 1,000 goal, goes from monochrome to colour and captures on celluloid the most explosive finishing ever seen. I bet he could even teach Brian Clough to walk on water!

He seems a Colossus on the field and yet, when I met him, I found myself looking down to meet his eyes.

He has been the most magnificent ambassador for the game, even when under immense pressure, and has set standards that will never be matched.

When he talks of his own incredible abilities, he disclaims all personal credit. Pele is firmly convinced that he was blessed with a divine gift.

"I feel my greatest skill is the ability to make something out of nothing," he said. "Of course you need speed, and balance of mind and body, but I have something else, an extra instinct God has given me. I see the ball, and others think there is no danger and, in two seconds, there is a goal.

"Eusebio is a great player, but he needs others around him. God has given me the ability to make something out of nothing, but that does not make me proud. It makes me humble, because I have to use his talent well. Aside from everything I do, there is always the hand of God. He made me a footballer, and keeps me a footballer."

Pele's God did more than that — he made him *the* footballer.

Denis Law – football's Max Miller.
(Allsport)

DENIS LAW
(Huddersfield, Manchester City, Torino, Manchester United and Scotland)

Denis Law was the Max Miller of the football field — a "cheeky chappy".

Little, quick, hot-tempered, cynical, he, more than any other British goalscorer, made his home in the six-yard box. He may have been frail, but he had a quick eye and was totally fearless.

143

Matt Busby said he had never seen Law's goals equalled "for sheer bravery", and I would agree. He made space out of nothing and, although there was not a spare ounce of flesh on him, could not be pushed off the ball.

He made the difficult look simple, adjusting to a ball coming at a strange angle and tucking it neatly into a corner without ever looking hurried.

There was always excessive flippancy and humour in the goals he scored, a cockiness, an inward grin that said: "I bet you didn't expect me to do that!" whenever he recovered a seemingly lost cause.

In season 1973-74, playing for Manchester City, he scored the goal that sent his beloved Manchester United plummeting into Division Two for the first time since 1938.

It was a back-heel flick, a natural reaction for a man who dedicated his life to goals of this nature, a throwaway effort, if you like, that caused a great catastrophe to befall the club he worshipped.

Law began to celebrate but then, realising what he had done, doubled up and put his head in his hands. It is the only time I've ever seen a striker wish he could take the ball from the net and pretend nothing had happened!

But it was too late, the goal sparked a riot and United were relegated.

Law played for Scotland in the World Cup that summer, but never kicked a ball in League football again.

IAN RUSH
(Chester, Liverpool and Wales)

Ian Rush is, quite simply, *the* striker of the 1980s. He emphasised this in 1983-84, when he scored the extraordinarily high total of 47 goals.

That he did it in a side like Liverpool's — brimful of scoring talent — is another tribute to the young Welshman's prowess.

He is the archetypal one-touch finisher. I would guess that, with 90 per cent of his goals, he provides only the finishing strike.

He has magnificent timing and speed, enabling him to meet the ball at just the right angle and time, and his improvement over the last few seasons has been colossal.

His general skill, and particularly his control, have come on by leaps and bounds. He is living proof that you *can* learn to be a goalscorer.

He will work tirelessly at his game, and never be satisfied until he has achieved perfection in a goalscoring capacity.

"There is always room for improvement," he said. "I got five in a game one season, so my next target is six! I won't be happy until I take every chance that comes my way."

He came pretty close to perfection when scoring a hat-trick in Liverpool's 3-1 win over Aston Villa in January 1984.

For his first he outpaced Villa's Gary Williams — despite giving the defender a good yard start — to run onto Mark Lawrenson's long through-pass. His second was a spectacular left-foot volley, hit first time across goalkeeper Nigel Spink and into the far corner of the net. He completed probably the most devastating hat-trick I have seen, by pouncing on Alan Evans's poor back-pass and perfectly lobbing the advancing Spink.

Tony Barton, the Villa manager, said after

Ian Rush, the modern Greaves.
(Hailey Sports)

Rush's one-man show (televised live by BBC): "He's out on his own as the best striker in Britain, if not Europe. He's quick off the mark, gets in front of defenders so well, and is lethal anywhere near the penalty area."

Kevin Keegan, another great goal-getter and Anfield hero, described Rush as "the best finisher I have seen."

Not much more needs to be said.

KENNY DALGLISH
(Celtic, Liverpool and Scotland)

I am sure Denis Law — "The King" to his fans — will not mind his record of 30 goals for Scotland being equalled by Kenny Dalglish.

He surely could not have objected to the way in which the Liverpool man did it, in the World Cup qualifying tie against Spain at Hampden Park in November 1984.

Fed by Liverpool team-mate Steve Nicol, Dalglish cut inside and left two Spanish defenders trailing, before beating goalkeeper Luis Arconada with a marvellous left-foot shot. Scotland won the match 3-1.

Now in his mid-30s, and approaching his 100th appearance for his country — he has already played more than 30 games more than any other Scotsman — he hasn't slowed a jot.

Dalglish is one player I could watch every day of the week. He has brought a new dimension to the art of turning the centre-half and is a brilliant striker of the ball.

Even now, as age has forced a move into more of a midfield role, he still has a magnificent featherlight touch and a youthful enthusiasm for taking men on.

Dalglish has always managed to look a good five years younger than he is, and it is impossible to think that he may soon be retiring from the game.

Watching Dalglish, and his former Liverpool partner Graeme Souness, I am always astonished that Scotland have never had greater success at international level.

Kenny still gets enormous joy from scoring — a fact that radiates from the pitch to the terraces — and is a great entertainer as well as a goalscorer; it's not often the two go together.

He has been immensely loyal to each of his

clubs, Celtic and Liverpool, when it is obvious that he could long ago have deserted for foreign parts.

No less a man than Bob Paisley, the former Liverpool boss, with a record of achievements second to none, said of Kenny: "He is one of the greatest, if not the best, Liverpool player there has ever been."

Coming from a man who played alongside Billy Liddell, trained Roger Hunt and Ian St. John and managed Kevin Keegan, Graeme Souness and Ian Rush, that is some praise.

UWE SEELER
(West Germany)

Few people remember Seeler as an out-and-out great goalscorer, yet one look at his record for West Germany says it all. In 72 matches, he scored 43 goals; only Muller's achievement of 67 goals in 62 games stands higher.

Seeler, a little, stocky man, was a phenomenal header of the ball, who had great jumping power and seemed to fly through the air to meet crosses.

Not even an operation to insert an artificial achilles tendon could deter him, and he starred in four World Cups.

He scored goals that would have made Dixie Dean proud, and was one of the first modern-type forwards — busy and bustling, dragging people about in the area and getting anything from long range headers, to tap-ins in the six-yard box and 30 yard blasters.

He had no weaknesses, and appeared to be a very proud man, proud of his country and his own abilities.

Although there were some magnificent British players about in my younger days, I never missed a chance to see Seeler live or on

*Kenny Dalglish – I
could watch him every
day.*
(Allsport)

television. One of my most exciting exper-
iences was watching an international in his
home country, being among 100,000 frantic
fans chanting: "UWE! UWE! UWE!" in homage to their hero and captain.

That Seeler skippered West Germany is
further tribute to his remarkable strength of
character. As a rule, goalscorers are too in-
sular, too single-minded, too selfish to fulfil
this role. They concentrate on their own job,
and don't have the time for team matters.

Yet Seeler's dedication to his country was
such that he could break that pattern. He was
a bundle of energy who, at the height of his
career, had such enthusiasm that everyone
looked lazy by comparison.

Of the current German stars, only Karl-
Heinz Rummenigge comes close, except
Rummenigge is not as strong in the air.

Seeler had excellent control, a fine shot
and could lay a ball off and then dart for the
return more explosively than any other forward of his age.

Although many still recall his supposedly
"impossible" back-headed goal against England in the 1970 World Cup Finals in Leon —
ridiculously dismissed as "lucky" by some
British correspondents — it is strange that
Seeler has never been given the lavish praise
afforded many lesser foreign internationals
by the British public.

TOSTAO
(Brazil)

In addition to attracting admiration because
of his tremendous talent, Tostao was the sort
of forward who tugged on your heart-strings.

He was like everyone's favourite teddy-bear
— the one with only one eye, an arm
hanging-off, threadbare and looking as if it
needed a good meal.

In the pre-match warm-up you'd easily mistake him for the mascot. Yet when the tracksuits had been collected, the toss decided and ends changed, he kicked off alongside the Peles, the Jairzinhos and the Gersons.

Tostao did only have one eye. An accident in training detached a retina and only a series of operations in Houston, Texas, enabled him to play in the 1970 World Cup. Unfortunately, the injury forced premature retirement in 1973, at the age of 26. But he had still done enough up to then to prove himself worthy of a place alongside the all-time greats.

He had such a lazy style, that he could leave a defence spellbound with barely one touch. He would nip off the centre-half, kill the ball and then turn, facing his marker with his foot slightly over the ball. He resembled a cat poised to pounce when hunting.

Then, a half smile broke across his face as he stared his opponent coldly in the eye. It was as if he were saying: "Well, what are you going to do now?"

As the unfortunate defender moved, he would quickly lay the ball off and dart into the six yard area.

Some talk of players possessing the ability to "stop a game," but Tostao really could do that. He would get the ball, and no-one would move. They simply hadn't a clue about his intentions.

Even Pele couldn't do that. Tostao would roll his studs over the ball while gently chastising his opponents' ineptitude.

His most delicate touch was to stop dead on the half-turn, dummy to pass the way he was facing, then suddenly back-heel the ball to a man making a run behind him. It was a sort of sixth-sense and, having done it, he would turn round to his marker with a reproachful look that said: "You didn't fall for that old trick, did you?"

But it wasn't just showing off on Tostao's part — there was a purpose to every move he made.

And, although he could also play the simple stuff — brilliantly — he remained basically a poacher in the box. He lived for tap-ins and, while Pele would get the headlines with a 20-yard volley, Tostao would pass almost unnoticed with two simple goals.

ALAN GILZEAN
(Tottenham and Scotland)

Many people will be surprised to see Alan Gilzean among my "top ten" goalscorers, yet he had a grace and poise that has never been equalled — in fact, he was the nearest thing to a ballerina on a football field.

Although Alan's goalscoring record is less than one every three games, and his total of caps for Scotland a mere 22, both figures belie his tremendous ability. The *quality* of his goals was outstanding. It is nothing short of a travesty that he should have gone so unrewarded by his country.

Dave Mackay, who captained both Spurs and Scotland, once said: "When I look at some of the players who have worn the navy blue jersey ahead of 'Gillie', it is ridiculous.

"Alan proved his talent week in, week out, against top-class opposition at home and abroad. Yet for Scotland he was always the one to be left out after a bad result. I have never understood that — and never will."

Tall and slim, with a strange high-stepping run, Gilzean might not have been the quickest of forwards, but his flicks and deft touches were unforgettable.

With his head or his boot, his touch was so delicate that you felt the average clumsy centre-half would smash him to pieces. Yet Gilzean never got caught.

His chest control, too, was brilliant, which helped him enormously in his role as "target man" or "feed."

As his Scotland team-mate Denis Law pointed out: "Alan was ideal for me. I liked to play quick and sharp, and he was the best partner I have ever had for doing the one-touch stuff. There was no-one better for allowing you that extra yard of space.

"Had he represented his country more often, I feel sure we would have been a better team."

But perhaps Gilzean's one overriding quality was his heading — he was a master in the air in the six-yard box.

West Ham's Martin Peters was known as "The Ghost" because of his ability to slip in at the near post — but really the nickname was tailor-made for Gilzean. His timing was immaculate. He would glide in, jump, and meet the ball for the perfect delicate flick into goal.

Then he would wheel away triumphantly with that strange high-stepping action.

Even Peters, a team-mate at Spurs, admits Gilzean was the best.

"I can remember playing Carlisle in the FA Cup in 1971-72," he said, "and someone hit a near post cross. We were all waiting for Martin Chivers to get on the end of it, when 'Gillie' appeared from almost nowhere to head the ball into the net.

"It was a fantastic goal. The best header I have ever seen."

All these strikers have had one thing in common — the ability to spin and accelerate exceptionally quickly. The power to do this is created, not so much by natural speed, but by achieving a low centre of gravity.

This brings me back to the subject of the

goalscorer's crouch. Many centre-halves are easily pushed over because their centre of gravity is somewhere between their chest and stomach, making them top-heavy and not properly balanced.

Centre-forwards, however, should crouch so that the centre of gravity is right in the crotch, in the middle of the body, making them more stable, almost unmovable.

It might seem funny, but you'll notice that all goalscorers have a particular walk: they stoop, rotate at the shoulders and roll their hips, not unlike John Wayne.

They play with bent legs, with hollowed backs, and look almost like monkeys!

Go through the whole of the Football League and you'll rarely find a striker with a straight-back (Kerry Dixon and Graeme Sharp are the exceptions, being predominantly aerial men).

Indeed, if you are short, squat but athletic, and have the ideal physique for judo or perhaps middleweight boxing, then you are the right build for a goalscorer!

After absorbing the lessons outlined in this book, I hope that you will have the necessary ability, too ... *get it, turn, shoot!*